SCOTT FORESMAN

Art

Rebecca Brooks, Ph.D.
Program Author

PEARSON

Scott
Foresman

Editorial Offices: Glenview, Illinois • Parsippany, New Jersey • New York, New York

Sales Offices: Needham, Massachusetts • Duluth, Georgia • Glenview, Illinois • Coppell, Texas • Sacramento, California • Mesa, Arizona

Program *Consultants*

Christopher Adejumo, Ph.D.
Associate Professor
    Visual Art Studies
    University of Texas
    Austin, Texas

Doug Blandy, Ph.D.
Professor and Director
    Arts and Administration Program
    Institute for Community Arts
        and Studies
    University of Oregon
    Eugene, Oregon

Georgia Collins, Ph.D.
Professor Emeritus
    College of Fine Arts
    University of Kentucky
    Lexington, Kentucky

Deborah Cooper, M.Ed.
Coordinating Director of Arts Education
    Curriculum and Instruction
    Charlotte-Mecklenburg Schools
    Charlotte, North Carolina

Sandra M. Epps, Ph.D.
Multicultural Art Education Consultant
    New York, New York

Mary Jo Gardere
Multi-Arts Specialist
    Eladio Martinez Learning Center
    Dallas, Texas

Carlos G. Gómez, M.F.A.
Professor of Fine Art
    University of Texas at Brownsville
        and Texas Southmost College
    Brownsville, Texas

Kristina Lamour, M.F.A.
Assistant Professor
    The Art Institute of Boston at
        Lesley University
    Boston, Massachusetts

Melinda M. Mayer, Ph.D.
Assistant Professor
    School of Visual Arts
    University of North Texas
    Denton, Texas

Robyn Montana Turner, Ph.D.
Author and University Teacher
    Austin, Texas

Contributing Authors

Sara A. Chapman, M,Ed.
Coordinator, Visual Arts Program
Alief Independent School District, Houston, TX

James M. Clarke, M,Ed.
Executive Director, Texas Coalition for Quality Arts Education, Houston, TX

Reviewers

Studio Reviewers

Judy Abbott, *Art Educator*
Allison Elementary School
Austin Independent
School District
Austin, Texas

Lin Altman, *Art Educator*
Cedar Creek
Elementary School
Eanes Independent
School District
Austin, Texas

Geral T. Butler,
Art Educator (Retired)
Heritage High School
Lynchburg City Schools
Lynchburg, Virginia

Dale Case,
Elementary Principal
Fox Meadow Elementary
School
Nettleton School District
Jonesboro, Arkansas

Deborah McLouth,
Art Educator
Zavala Elementary School
Austin Independent
School District
Austin, Texas

Patricia Newman,
Art Educator
Saint Francis Xavier School
Archdiocese of Chicago
La Grange, Illinois

Nancy Sass, *Art Educator*
Cambridge Elementary
School
Alamo Heights Independent
School District
San Antonio, Texas

Sue Spiva Telle, *Art Educator*
Woodridge Elementary
School
Alamo Heights Independent
School District
San Antonio, Texas

Cari Washburn, *Art Educator*
Great Oaks Elementary School
Round Rock Independent
School District
Round Rock, Texas

Critic Readers

Celeste Anderson
Roosevelt Elementary School
Nampa, Idaho

Mary Jo Birkholz
Wilson Elementary School
Janesville, Wisconsin

Mary Jane Cahalan
Mitzi Bond Elementary
School
El Paso, Texas

Cindy Collar
Cloverleaf Elementary School
Cartersville, Georgia

Yvonne Days
St. Louis Public Schools
St. Louis, Missouri

Shirley Dickey
Creative Art Magnet School
Houston, Texas

Ray Durkee
Charlotte Performing
Arts Center
Punta Gorda, Florida

Sue Flores-Minick
Bryker Woods
Elementary School
Austin, Texas

Denise Jennings
Fulton County Schools
Atlanta, Georgia

Alicia Lewis
Stevens Elementary School
Houston, Texas

James Miller
Margo Elementary School
Weslaco, Texas

Marta Olson
Seattle Public Schools
Seattle, Washington

Judy Preble
Florence Avenue School
Irvington, New Jersey

Tonya Roberson
Oleson Elementary School
Houston, Texas

Andrew Southwick
Edgewood Independent
School District
San Antonio, Texas

Nita Ulaszek
Audelia Creek
Elementary School
Dallas, Texas

Tessie Varthas
Office of Creative and
Public Art
Philadelphia, Pennsylvania

Penelope Venola
Spurgeon Intermediate School
Santa Ana, California

Elizabeth Willett
Art Specialist
Fort Worth, Texas

Contents

Unit 1

The Elements of Art 14

Vincent van Gogh. *Still Life: Vase with Twelve Sunflowers,* 1888.

Unit 2

The Principles of Design...................62

Artist unknown, Mayan. *Urn or Brazier in the Shape of a Priest,* pre-Columbian.

Gil Mayers. *Time Piece.* Mixed media.

Unit 3

Art Media and Techniques 102

Postnik Yakovlev, architect. *St. Basil's Cathedral (Petrovsky Cathedral)*, 1555–1561.

Unit 4
The Creative Process.......................154

Diego Rivera. *Delfina Flores*, 1927.

Unit 5
Styles in Art History.......................198

Artist unknown. *Pictographic tablet from Jamdat Nasr, near Kish, Iraq,* ca. 3000 B.C.

Artist unknown, Japanese. *Kimono,* 20th century.

Unit 6
Careers in Art 250

Ansel Adams. *The Tetons-Snake River.*
Wyoming, 1942.

Liliana Bonomi. *"Elaios" Oil Server.*

6

Michael Bartalos. *Design Quarterly #166.* Fiftieth anniversary Issue.

Maya Lin. *Women's Table,* 1993.

Introduction to Visual Art

Art may be anything from a song on the radio to a play performed onstage. The subject of this book is **visual art.** Painting, sculpture, and drawing are all forms of visual art. Other visual art forms include ceramics, weaving, photography, and architecture. Human beings have been using visual art as a method of communication for more than thirty thousand years. In fact, the use of images for communication is older than the use of words.

Learning to communicate through visual art involves more than making artworks. It also involves observing and thinking about the art that fills your environment in new ways. For instance, have you ever considered the everyday objects and images you see as works of art? The cars on the street, the newest shopping mall, and the special effects of today's movies are all designed and completed by career artists. Like sculptors and painters, these artists rely on some basic visual arts concepts that you will read about in this book.

Fine artworks, everyday artworks, and images from the natural environment are all around us. These images are a part of our **visual culture.** Learning about the visual arts will help you to explore this culture. It will promote a greater appreciation and ability to communicate with the world of visual art.

Georgia O'Keeffe. *Apple Family II*, ca. 1920. Oil on canvas, 8 ⅛ by 10 ⅛ inches. Georgia O'Keeffe Musuem, Santa Fe, NM.

Art Criticism

Artworks provide an opportunity for visual communication between the artist and the viewer. The role of the viewer is as important as the artwork itself and the artist who made it. It is the viewer that gives the art experience purpose and life. Just as artists practice and work with materials, tools, and techniques to create artworks, you can develop your skills in observing and understanding them.

Art criticism is the process of looking at works of art in a guided and logical way. This four-stage process can help you organize your thoughts about artworks and increase your understanding, enjoyment, and appreciation of them.

Examine the artwork on this page as you read about the four levels of art criticism and answer the questions.

Describe is the basic information about the artwork. This may include who made it, what materials were used, and the artwork's size and subject matter.

- When was the artwork made?
- What medium did the artist use?
- What objects do you recognize?

Analyze is a tool for looking at how an artwork is put together. This includes how the artist used colors, lines, or shapes, where they are used, and how they relate to one another in the artwork.

- What colors seem most important?
- How has the artist changed some of the figures and objects?
- How did the artist show that some objects are farther away than others?

Interpret is your opinion about what the artist is saying or expressing in the artwork, and how the previous steps relate to the artist's message.

- What do you think the artist was expressing about the Red Cross?
- Why do you think the artist chose to paint the subject in a non-realistic way?
- How do you think the artist feels about the subject? Why do you think so?

Judge is your opportunity to decide whether you think the work has value and whether the artist was successful in communicating his or her ideas.

- How well do you think the artwork reflects the time and culture in which it was made?
- In what area of a museum might you find this artwork? Explain.
- What, if anything, would you change about this artwork? Why?

You will learn how to apply these four stages of art criticism in each lesson of this book. This process will help you evaluate and appreciate the artworks of others, as well as your own works of art.

William H. Johnson. *Red Cross Nurses Handing Out Wool for Knitting,* ca. 1942. Gouache and pen and ink with pencil on paper, 17 3/8 by 21 7/8 inches. Smithsonian American Art Museum, Washington, D.C.

Visit a Museum

Many communities in the United States have **art museums,** structures designed to protect and exhibit artworks. Observing a work of art in a museum is different from seeing it reproduced on a page. A firsthand view allows you to experience the artwork as it left the artist's hands. You see its actual size and intensity, and you can closely examine its physical details from several angles.

Art museums are as varied as the artworks they exhibit. Some museums, such as the Guggenheim, have extensive permanent collections. They display artworks of varying media from different eras throughout history. Other art museums focus on a specific medium, such as clay, or artworks representing a particular style or culture. The Nedra Matteucci's Fenn Galleries in Santa Fe, for example, exhibits artworks by modern and historic Taos and Santa Fe artists.

All works of art express ideas that are intended to spark a response. Art museums provide a space and a mood to bring the artists' visions to viewers.

Nedra Matteucci's Fenn Galleries, Santa Fe, New Mexico.

The Guggenheim Museum, located in the heart of New York City, was designed by well-known American architect Frank Lloyd Wright. The building itself is a spectacular artwork.

Interior of the Guggenheim Museum.

Art museums employ many people who work behind the scenes to display, protect, and care for the artworks. Others provide information and education to visitors.

A **docent** greets visitors to the museum and guides them through the exhibitions. The docent's job is to answer questions about the artworks, artists, and the museum. Some docents are trained volunteers.

A **curator** selects the artworks for an exhibition and decides where they should be placed. Curators may travel the world looking for artworks to acquire for a museum's permanent collection. They also borrow artworks from other museums' collections to create temporary and special exhibitions. A curator often works with the community to determine the museum's needs.

A **conservator** studies ways to protect artworks from damage. Some conservators restore artworks that have become damaged by age or decay. They work to preserve artworks so that future generations can enjoy them.

Museum Etiquette

When visiting an art museum, remember to:
- Obey all posted signs.
- Talk softly so that you do not disturb others. Loud voices carry in museum galleries.
- Never touch an artwork. Stay at least an arm's length away from artwork.
- Do not walk in front of someone who is viewing an artwork.
- Do not bring food and drink near the artworks.
- Do not take photographs. Flash photography can damage works of art.
- Do not carry backpacks or book bags. Bulky objects can swing and bump into works of art.

Make a Sketchbook Journal

Artists fill the blank pages of their sketchbooks with drawings and words that reflect their observations, imaginations, experiences, and ideas. It is the place where artists experiment, make changes, and practice techniques. It is also the perfect place to take notes and plan art projects.

Follow these steps to make your own Sketchbook Journal.

Materials

- ✓ cardboard (two 10" × 13" sheets)
- ✓ construction paper
- ✓ drawing paper (9" × 12" sheets)
- ✓ fabric (two 12" × 15" pieces)
- ✓ hammer and nail ⚠
- ✓ scissors, tape, glue ⚠
- ✓ raffia, yarn, or twine

1 Use scissors to score one piece of cardboard one inch from the left edge to make a front cover that will fold.

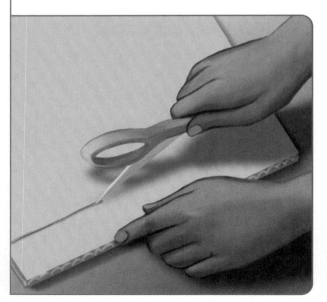

2 Cut two pieces of fabric one inch larger than your cardboard. Pull the fabric tight and wrap it around the cardboard. Tape the edges to the back side. Glue construction paper over the taped edges to cover them.

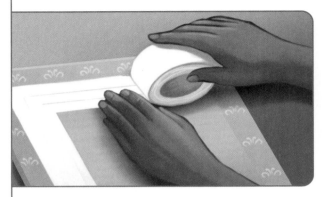

3 Use a hammer and nail to punch holes in a zigzag pattern along the spine of the sketchbook. Use your cover as a guide to punch holes through a stack of drawing paper.

4 Weave raffia, yarn, or twine in and out of the holes to bind the pages together.

Make a Portfolio

Many artists keep their artworks in a portfolio. This allows them to protect and transport the artworks.

Follow these steps to make your own portfolio.

Materials

- ✓ posterboard
- ✓ tape
- ✓ scissors ⚠
- ✓ yarn or twine
- ✓ button
- ✓ stapler ⚠
- ✓ markers or oil pastels

1 Staple or tape two sheets of posterboard along three sides.

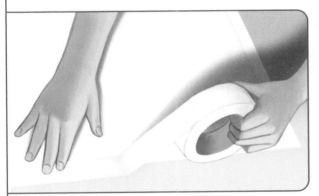

2 Cut a six-inch piece of posterboard the width of the open side. Tape the piece to the back of the open side, fold over the top, and crease it to create a flap.

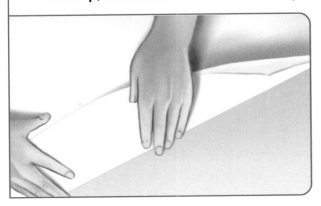

3 Staple a five-inch piece of yarn or twine to the flap and attach a button to the open side as a wraparound tie closure.

4 Design your portfolio using markers, oil pastels, or a collage technique. Use your imagination! Remember to write your name on your portfolio.

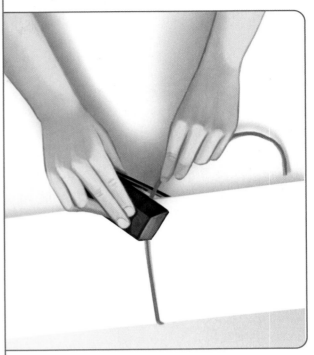

Leonardo da Vinci. *Mona Lisa,* 1503–1506. Oil on wood, 30 ¼ by 21 inches.
Musée de Louvre, Paris.

Unit 1

The Elements of Art

Do you recognize this famous painting? It was painted by Leonardo da Vinci about five centuries ago. There are objects of visual art such as this painting all around you—on walls, in museums, in public plazas. You see visual art in living rooms when you look at designer chairs and in movies as special visual effects.

To create visual art such as the *Mona Lisa,* artists use the elements of art, the basic parts and symbols of artworks. The seven **elements of art** include **line, shape, form, space, value, color,** and **texture.** Every artwork includes some of these elements, and many artworks include them all. The many ways in which artists have used and combined these elements make each artwork unique.

In this unit, you will discover more about each of the elements of art. You will also learn how, through your own observation and creativity, you can use these same seven elements to create your own works of art.

About *the Artist*

Leonardo da Vinci created paintings such as the famous *Mona Lisa,* but did you know that he also designed machinery? Read more about Leonardo's contributions to art and science on page 36.

Leonardo da Vinci. *Self-Portrait.*

Line

In the language of art, a **line** is the path left by a point moving across a surface. Line is one of the elements of art. You can make lines with a pencil, pen, crayon, marker, or paintbrush. You can scratch them into clay or carve them into wood or plastic. Even your signature is a series of lines. Lines can be thick or thin, and they can be continuous or broken. They can be straight or curved, wavy or jagged.

Types of Lines

vertical line

horizontal line

diagonal line

zigzag line

thick line

thin line

broken line

continuous line

curved line

What types of lines do you see in nature?

What types of lines do you see in human-made objects?

Edvard Munch. *The Scream,* 1893. Tempera and pastel on board, 35 ½ by 28 ⅓ inches. The National Gallery, Oslo, Norway.

Using Lines to Express

Norwegian artist Edvard Munch (1863–1944) used a variety of lines to paint this famous artwork. Notice the kinds of lines Munch used and what they express. Find **vertical lines,** which go up and down and can express strength and height. Find **horizontal lines,** which are parallel to the horizon. **Parallel lines** are the same distance apart and never intersect one another. Where do you see parallel lines in this painting? Now find **diagonal lines,** which may slant in any direction. They appear unstable, suggesting motion. What kinds of lines make it look as if the air is vibrating with the sound of the scream?

Sketchbook Journal

Make a chart of lines by sketching the kinds of lines that you observe in your classroom, at home, and outdoors. Note where you saw each line and what made it interesting or unusual. Use a variety of tools to make the lines. Does one tool do a better job than others of showing a particular kind of line?

17

Lines *in Motion*

Thomas Hart Benton. *Going West,* 1934. Lithograph, 12 5/16 by 23 3/8 inches. Amon Carter Museum, Fort Worth, Texas.

Why does the train seem to be moving?

Artists use the elements of art to suggest motion in artworks. In this print, Thomas Hart Benton (1889–1975) used lines to show the motion and direction of the train. Notice these details:

- The front edge of the train and the lines separating the cars are diagonal, making the train look as if it is moving toward the left edge of the artwork.
- The poles seem to lean back, exaggerating the forward motion of the train.

Actual and Implied Lines

Some of the lines Benton used to show motion are **actual lines** —lines you can actually see. Others are **implied lines.** You cannot actually see implied lines, but you imagine that they are there. They are suggested by the placement of actual lines, shapes, and colors. Look closely at the train track behind the nearest pole. What kind of line did Benson use to show this part of the track? Where do you notice other implied lines in the artwork?

Technique Tip

Diagonal Lines

Practice using various drawing tools to create diagonal lines. Use each tool in different ways. For example, draw one line using the tip of the tool and another using the edge. Notice how different lines can suggest different kinds of movement.

Studio 1

Draw with Lines

Use what you have learned about lines to draw a vehicle in motion.

Materials

- ✓ 12" × 18" white drawing paper
- ✓ pencil and sketchbook (optional)
- ✓ black crayon or colored pencil

1 Think of a vehicle, such as a ship, a skateboard, or a car. Visualize it in motion.

2 Sketch some ideas with a pencil. Then, draw your subject on the paper using black crayon or colored pencil.

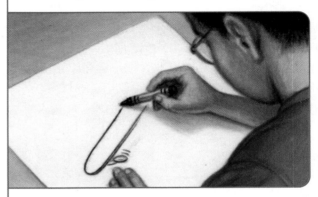

3 Use a variety of actual and implied lines to show motion. They might be diagonal, zigzag, or curved lines.

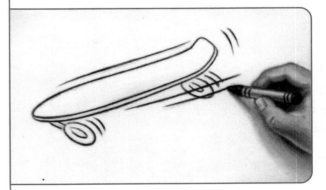

Review and Reflect

- Describe the kinds of lines you used in your drawing.
- Point out the lines that show motion best. What makes them work?
- How does drawing the object in motion change how you think about it?
- How would you show motion and direction differently next time?

Shape

Shape, an element of art, is a flat, two-dimensional area with height and width. A shape may or may not have an edge or an outline. What shapes can you think of that do not have an outline? You could probably name many objects simply by their shape. For example, in the photograph below, you can tell that the object is a palm tree from the shape of its shadow.

Types of Shapes

circle

square

rectangle

oval

triangle

organic

Look for shapes in the natural environment.

Geometric shapes are most often found in the human-made environment.

Georgia O'Keeffe. *Blue and Green Music,* 1919. Oil on canvas, 32 3/4 by 18 7/8 inches. The Art Institute of Chicago, Chicago, IL.

Expressing with Shapes

American artist Georgia O'Keeffe (1887–1986) painted *Blue and Green Music,* using both geometric and organic shapes. **Geometric** shapes are precise, mathematical shapes, such as circles, squares, and rectangles. **Organic** shapes are irregular and are often found in nature. Find the organic and geometric shapes in the painting. Remember, the title of the artwork is *Blue and Green Music.* What kind of musical note or passage do you think each shape suggests? Why do you think O'Keeffe gave this title to her artwork?

Sketchbook Journal

On a walk in your neighborhood, sketch a variety of shapes that you see in nature, such as a leaf, a stone, and a cloud. Next to each sketch, draw the geometric shape that most closely matches each organic shape. Notice the similarities and differences between the two shapes.

Henri Matisse. *The Horse, the Rider, and the Clown, Plate V from the Jazz Series,* 1947. Color stencil print, 25 5/8 by 16 9/16 inches. The Herbert F. Johnson Museum of Art, Cornell University, Ithaca, NY.

What kinds of shapes can you identify in this artwork?

Artists use the elements of art to express feelings and moods. In this collage, French artist Henri Matisse (1869–1954) used shapes to suggest the energy and fun of a circus. Notice these details:

- The horse is composed of both geometric and organic shapes. The shapes in the border are organic and lively.
- The shapes create implied lines. There are no two shapes that are exactly the same.
- The different shapes create the sense of noise and excitement associated with a circus.

Filled-in and Cutout Shapes

Matisse used a combination of filled-in shapes and cutout shapes to create this artwork. Look closely at the yellow shape in the lower left-hand corner. Is it yellow paper with a black shape glued on top, or is it black paper with a yellow shape glued on top? What is the background color of the collage? Notice the other shapes in the collage to help you discover the answers.

Technique Tip

Unwanted Pencil Marks

Sometimes after you sketch a shape, and then cut it out, some of the unwanted pencil lines remain. To make removing the lines easier, sketch very lightly with the pencil. A pencil eraser will work to remove any remaining lines, but an art gum eraser leaves fewer marks. To prevent creasing or tearing, erase from the center outward.

Studio 2

Make Shadow Shapes

Use what you have learned about shapes to draw and cut out shadow shapes.

Materials

- ✓ 12" × 18" heavy white drawing paper
- ✓ 12" × 18" black construction paper
- ✓ 3 objects of different shapes
- ✓ lamp or other light source
- ✓ colored chalk or oil pastels
- ✓ scissors or cutting tool ⚠
- ✓ glue

1 Use a light source and arrange three small objects so that they cast shadows on the drawing paper. Use pastels to color in the shadow shapes.

2 Move the objects to create new shadows. Allow shapes to overlap. This time, cut out the shapes created by the shadows. Repeat steps 1 and 2.

3 Glue the drawing paper to black construction paper so the cutout shapes show clearly.

Review and Reflect

- Describe the kinds of shapes you drew and cut out.
- How did the objects you used help create the shapes?
- What feelings or moods does your artwork express?
- Which shapes do you like best? Why? What would you do differently next time?

Lesson 3

Form

As an element of art, **form** means an object that has three dimensions: height, width, and depth. A circle is a shape; a ball is a form. Because a form has three dimensions, you must look at its front, back, sides, top, and bottom to fully view it. Larger, empty forms such as a building, can even be viewed from the inside.

Types of Forms

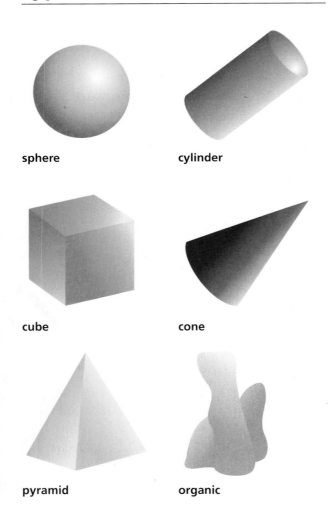

sphere

cylinder

cube

cone

pyramid

organic

Where do you see forms in nature?

Some forms in nature are very similar to geometric forms.

24

Michael O'Keefe. *Unfolding II,* 2001. Faceted, dichroic glass sculpture, on an oblong base, with frosted edges, 9 by 15 inches. L. H. Selman, Ltd., Santa Cruz, CA.

Henry Moore. *Two-Piece Reclining Figure: Points,* 1969–1970. Bronze, 89 3/8 by 147 1/8 by 72 7/8 inches. Hirshhorn Museum and Sculpture Garden, Smithsonian Institution, Washington, D.C.

Geometric and Organic Forms

These artworks by Michael O'Keefe (1947–) and Henry Moore (1898–1986) illustrate the two basic kinds of forms: **geometric forms** and **organic forms.** O'Keefe used geometric forms to create *Unfolding II.* These forms are a three-dimensional version of which geometric shape? Now look at Moore's *Two-Piece Reclining Figure: Points.* Moore used organic shapes to show a figure in a reclining position. Notice how the two artists used different kinds of forms to create a different approach to their subjects.

Sketchbook Journal

Make sketches of a variety of geometric and organic shapes you see in both the natural and human-made environments. Then sketch each shape as a form. Experiment with ways to show a third dimension, such as adding lines and shading.

Expressing *Through Form*

Evaline Sellors. *Winter (Sleeping Fawn),* 1947. Limestone, 6 ½ by 9 ½ inches. Collection of the Modern Art Museum of Fort Worth, Fort Worth, Texas.

The simple details in this sculpture help reveal the animal's form.

American artist Evaline Sellors (1907–1995) made this sculpture of a sleeping fawn. A **sculpture** is an artwork made by modeling, carving, or joining materials to make a three-dimensional form. Notice these details about Sellors's use of form:

- The sculpture is carved from a small block of limestone.
- The form of the fawn is an organic form.
- Sellors used very little detail, yet you can still tell that the animal is a fawn.

Actual and Simulated Forms

A real fawn and the sculpture of the fawn are **actual forms** that have height, width, and depth. You can go around them both. However, the *photograph* of the fawn sculpture above has only two dimensions. This illusion of three dimensions on a two-dimensional surface is called **simulated form.** You can tell by looking at the image that the sculpture is a three-dimensional object. What clues in the photograph tell you this?

Technique Tip

Working with Clay

If you are unable to complete a clay project in one class period, be sure to keep the clay moist until you get back to it. To do this, use damp—not wet—paper towels and wrap your clay piece thoroughly. Then cover the entire piece with plastic and seal it well. If it dries out at all, try applying very small amounts of water to make it workable again.

Studio 3

Make a Clay Animal Form

Use what you have learned about form to make a simple animal form.

Materials

✓ drawing paper
✓ pictures of animals
✓ pencil and eraser
✓ black crayon
✓ ruler
✓ 3" × 7" × 4" block of self-hardening or ceramic clay
✓ clay tools

1 Draw the outline of an animal within a 3" × 7" area of the drawing paper.

2 Use a crayon to show on your drawing how you will carve the clay to show the animal's form and defining details.

3 Carve your animal from the block of clay, using your drawing as a guide. Be sure to carve all sides.

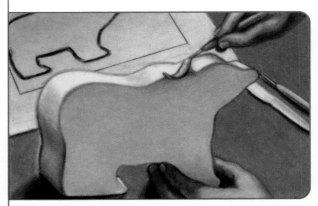

Review and Reflect

- Describe your sculpture.
- How did you choose which details to include and which ones to leave out?
- How does your sculpture express how you feel about the animal you chose?
- What title will you give your animal sculpture? Why?

Space

As an element of art, **space** means an area that may be empty or full, nearby or far away, huge or tiny. Space that is full or occupied by an object is called **positive space.** The empty space around the object is called **negative space.** A shape or a form may be negative space or positive space. In the photograph below, what part is the negative space, and what part is the positive space?

Auguste Rodin. *The Cathedral,* original stone version executed in 1908, cast 1955. Bronze, 25 by 12 ⅔ by 13 ⅓ inches. Musée Rodin, Paris, France.

Describe the positive space in this sculpture.

Identify the positive and negative space in these photographs.

Horace Pippin. *Man on a Park Bench,* 1946. Oil on composite board. Pennsylvania Academy of Fine Arts, Philadelphia, PA.

The Illusion of Space

Artists often add interest to their artworks by creating the illusion of space, or depth. **Depth** includes the techniques of linear perspective and overlapping to give the illusion of space and distance on a two-dimensional plane or surface. **Overlapping** is the placement of one object in front of another. Notice how American artist Horace Pippin (1888–1946) created the illusion that some trees are farther away from the viewer than others. Describe other areas of the painting where the artist used overlapping. Where do you see positive and negative space?

Sketchbook Journal

Find a simple scene outdoors to practice creating depth, such as a park bench or tree. Sketch the object as it appears when you are fairly close. Sketch the same object as if it were much farther away. Then, use overlapping to sketch a large ball between the two objects.

Studio 4 Setup
Space *and Distance*

Anna Belle Lee Washington.
City Park, 1992. Oil on
canvas, 18 by 24 inches.
© Anna Belle Lee Washington.

The buildings in the background of this painting include less detail than the people
and objects in the foreground.

The use of space helps artists show depth
in two-dimensional artworks. Notice the
following details in this painting by Anna
Belle Lee Washington (1924–2000):

- Washington showed space by overlapping
  some objects over others. The trees overlap
  the buildings in the distance.
- The people closest to the viewer are larger
  than those farther away and overlap the
  objects behind them.

Layers of Space

In an artwork, the objects that appear
nearest the viewer are in the **foreground.**
They appear larger, are often near the bottom,
and are darker and brighter with more
detail. Objects that appear farthest away are
in the **background** and are smaller than
closer objects. Objects placed between
the foreground and background are in
the **middle ground.** They appear slightly
smaller than those in the foreground.

Technique Tip

Showing Distance
**Practice sketching an object as it
would appear in the foreground,
middle ground, and background.
Make the object in the foreground
larger, the object in the middle ground
slightly smaller, and the object in the
background smaller still. Make notes
about how overlapping the objects
helps give the illusion of space.**

Draw to Show Space

Use what you have learned about space to draw an outer space scene that shows depth and distance.

Materials

- ✓ pencil
- ✓ 12" × 18" drawing paper
- ✓ outer space photographs (optional)
- ✓ 12" × 18" black construction paper
- ✓ chalk or oil pastels

1 Use your imagination or a photograph to sketch an outer space scene. Show planets, moons, stars, or other objects nearby and in the distance.

2 Include objects in the foreground, middle ground, and background. Overlap some objects.

3 Redraw your sketch onto the black paper. Use chalk or oil pastels to enhance the illusion of depth and distance.

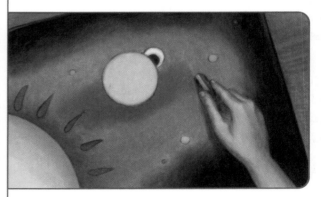

Review and Reflect

- Describe the objects in your drawing and the kinds of lines you used to draw them.
- Point out where you used overlapping. How does this help show space and depth?
- How would you explain the meaning of the illusion of depth in your drawing?
- How would you show depth and space differently next time?

Lesson 5

Space and Perspective

In the previous lesson, you learned how overlapping helps to create the illusion of depth in a two-dimensional artwork. In this lesson, you will discover the technique of linear perspective. **Linear perspective** allows artists to create the illusion of depth and distance using guidelines, like those in the illustration. These guidelines help artists position objects to appear near or far away. They also help them determine what size each object should be in relation to others, depending on where in space the object is placed. The line at which the sky and the ground meet is the **horizon line.** This line is usually at the viewer's eye level. All the lines meet, or converge, at the **vanishing point** located on the horizon line.

The diagonal lines of the buildings in the print by Nathaniel Currier (1813–1888) and James Ives (1824–1895) help lead the viewer's eye down the street of Broadway. The artists' use of detail in the foreground adds to the illusion of space and distance.

The next time you are outdoors, look down a long road or your neighborhood street as it goes into the distance. Notice where the actual and implied lines come together on the horizon.

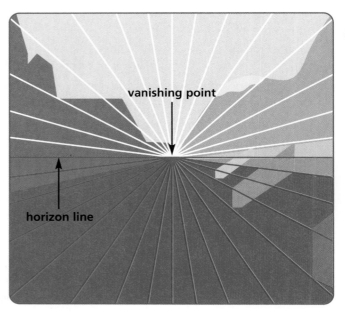

This illustration shows the guidelines of linear perspective.

Currier and Ives. *Broadway, from Cortland Street and Maiden Lane,* 1886. Lithograph. Private collection.

How is this artwork an example of linear perspective?

Albert Bierstadt. *Yosemite Falls,*
ca. 1865–1870. Oil on canvas.
Worcester Art Museum, Worcester, MA.

Atmospheric Perspective

Another technique artists use to show depth, space, and distance is **atmospheric perspective,** also called aerial perspective. In atmospheric perspective, objects in the foreground are often brighter and darker with more detail. Objects in the background are usually more muted and lighter. To add to the illusion of space, artists often include large portions of white in the background.

Notice Albert Bierstadt's (1830–1902) use of deeper colors in the foreground, making the rocks and trees in this painting of Yosemite Falls appear closer. The mountains and waterfall are muted and appear farthest away. Notice also how the large area of white gives the illusion of space and air.

Sketchbook Journal

Stand at one end of a long hallway at school or in another public building. Sketch the hallway using linear perspective techniques. Imagine the location of the vanishing point as the lines of the hallway converge. Draw the objects in the hallway, such as light fixtures, doorways, and lockers.

Ando Hiroshige. *Goyu
Station. Traveller Stopping
Girls: Tokaido series, No. 36,*
date unknown. Colored print,
14 by 9 inches. The Newark
Museum, Newark, NJ.

Where is the vanishing
point in this artwork?

Artists often use more than one technique
to show distance and space in the same
artwork. *Traveller Stopping Girls,* by Japanese
artist Ando Hiroshige (1797–1858), is a good
example. Notice these details:

- The two rows of buildings seem to meet
  at the vanishing point. The road seems
  to wind through the buildings and vanish
  in the distance.
- Objects in the foreground overlap others
  in the middle ground and background.

Kinds of Linear Perspective

The techniques of **one-point perspective**
include the use of a single vanishing point.
Diagonal or slanted lines converge at one
point on the horizon line or eye-level line.

Another type of linear perspective—
two-point perspective —includes the use
of two vanishing points. If you look down

two sides of a building from one corner,
the diagonal lines on either side of the
building seem to lead to two separate
vanishing points. What type of perspective
did Hiroshige use in this artwork? How
can you tell?

Technique Tip

Colored Pencils
When drawing with colored pencils,
the more pressure you apply, the
darker the color will be. Applying
too much pressure, however, can
cause the paper to tear. Tears can
also happen if the pencil has a very
sharp point. Wear the point down
slightly before drawing.

Draw to Show Perspective

Use what you have learned about perspective to draw a scene using one-point perspective.

Materials

- ✓ 12" × 18" white drawing paper
- ✓ pencil
- ✓ ruler
- ✓ colored pencils or water-based markers

1 Imagine that you are looking down a long road lined with houses or buildings. Use a ruler and a pencil to draw the road using linear perspective.

2 Use the principles of one-point perspective to add the houses or buildings, and other objects.

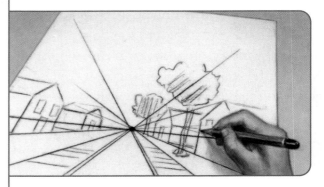

3 Use colored pencils or markers to add to the illusion of depth, showing more detail in closer objects than in those farther away.

Review and Reflect

- Describe the kinds of lines you used in your drawing?
- How do these lines help show linear perspective?
- What mood does the use of perspective give to your drawing?
- What techniques of linear perspective did you like using most? Why?

Meet *the Artist*

Leonardo da Vinci

Leonardo da Vinci was born in Italy on April 15, 1452. By the time he died, at age sixty-seven, he had explored the fields of art, science, geometry, anatomy, and philosophy. Along with artistic sketches and notes, Leonardo filled his notebooks with scientifically sound designs of flying machines long before such machines were possible. Da Vinci, known universally as Leonardo, is thought to have had the most complex imagination of all time.

Leonardo's only known self-portrait, drawn when he was about sixty years old.

"The most praiseworthy form of painting is the one that most resembles what it imitates." —LEONARDO

Leonardo da Vinci. *Self-Portrait.* Manuscript drawing, chalk on paper. Biblioteca Reale, Turin, Italy. Scala/Art Resource, New York.

A Long Life in Art

Leonardo was born in the village of Vinci, near Florence, Italy. When he was fifteen, he was apprenticed to the workshop of Andrea del Verrocchio, a well-known painter and sculptor in Florence.

In 1482, Leonardo left Florence for Milan, where he became the official artist to the duke. It was during this time that he painted the famous *Last Supper.* Leonardo did not return to Florence until 1500. He then painted several portraits, of which the best known is the *Mona Lisa.*

In 1516, Leonardo was appointed court painter to the King of France. He died in France three years later.

A Man of Mystery

Leonardo never married and had few close friends. He seemed obsessed with recording all of his creative thoughts, even those thoughts that challenged the accepted views of the day. Perhaps that was why he wrote some ideas in "mirror" writing— to discourage people from reading them. In order to read the words easily, you must hold them up to a mirror.

In some ways, despite all the writings and drawings he left behind, this genius creator was as mysterious as the smile he painted on the *Mona Lisa.*

Talk About It

Look back at the *Mona Lisa* on page 14. Where does Leonardo include fine details and where does he avoid them? Explain.

The Life of Leonardo

1450

1452
Leonardo born
on April 15

Andrea del Verrocchio

Becomes apprentice to
Andrea del Verrocchio
1467

1470

Enters service
of Duke Ludovico
Sforza in Milan
1482

Begins studies of flying
machines, nature,
anatomy, architecture
1485

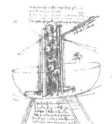
flying machine study

1490
Begins writing and
drawing in notebooks

1490

1495
Begins painting
Last Supper

the *Last Supper*

1500
Returns to Florence

1503
Begins painting
Mona Lisa

1510

King Francis I

Enters service of King
Francis I as court painter
1516

1519
Leonardo dies
in France

1530

Look *and Compare*

Portraits with Different Purposes

Leonardo da Vinci painted landscapes and filled notebooks with drawings of machines. But Leonardo was, above all, a painter of portraits. A **portrait** is a likeness of a person. Most portraits show the face of the subject in detail. Leonardo studied anatomy so that he could make his portraits lifelike.

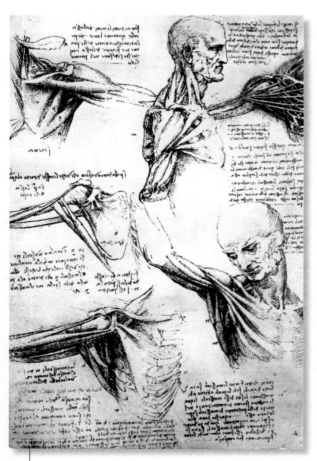

Leonardo da Vinci. *Study of the Human Anatomy,* ca. 1486.

A Court Portrait

Look at Leonardo's *Portrait of Cecilia Gallerani.* It is the portrait of a young woman who was a member of the court of the Duke of Milan. Leonardo painted it soon after he joined the court as a musician and artist. Then as now, portraits of members of royal households portrayed their subjects with beauty and dignity. How did Leonardo use line, shape, form, and space to fulfill his purpose as a court painter?

An Informal Portrait

Now look at *Head of Disheveled Young Girl.* Leonardo made this painting the same year, not for a royal patron but for himself. This painting may be a study, an informal artwork created to prepare for a more formal one. Perhaps it was a study for a later painting of Leda, a queen in Greek mythology. Leonardo used gouache to paint this portrait. Gouache is a water-based paint that dries faster than oil, allowing the artist little time to rework the painting.

This artwork appears incomplete or less formal compared to the painting above it. Leonardo used actual and implied lines to show the figure. Notice how these lines make her appear to blend into the background. He included more detail in the face, attracting the viewer's attention. In what other ways did Leonardo use line, shape, form, and space differently in the two artworks?

Leonardo da Vinci. *Portrait of Cecilia Gallerani (Lady with an Ermine),* 1490. Oil on walnut, 12 ⅓ by 15 ¾ inches. Czartoryski Museum, Cracow, Poland.

Leonardo da Vinci. *Head of Disheveled Young Girl (Leda),* ca. 1490. Umbra paint on panel, 10 ⅝ by 8 ¼ inches. National Gallery, Parma, Italy.

Compare & Contrast

- How are these portraits the same? How are they different?

- Compare these two portraits to Leonardo's *Mona Lisa* on page 14. Why do you think that *Mona Lisa* is the most famous of the three? What sets her apart?

Value

As an element of art, **value** is the lightness or darkness of a color. Notice how white is the lightest value and black is the darkest value in the artwork and photograph. The values between white and black are various degrees of gray. Transitions between different values help artists create a convincing illusion of form on a two-dimensional surface. Value is also an important element in helping artists show space, depth, and distance in artworks.

Which areas have the lightest and darkest values?

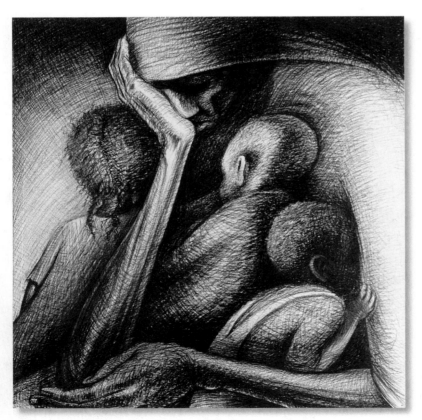

John Biggers. *The Cradle,* 1950. Conte crayon on paper, 22 3/8 by 21 1/2 inches. The Museum of Fine Arts, Houston, TX.

blending

stippling

hatching

cross-hatching

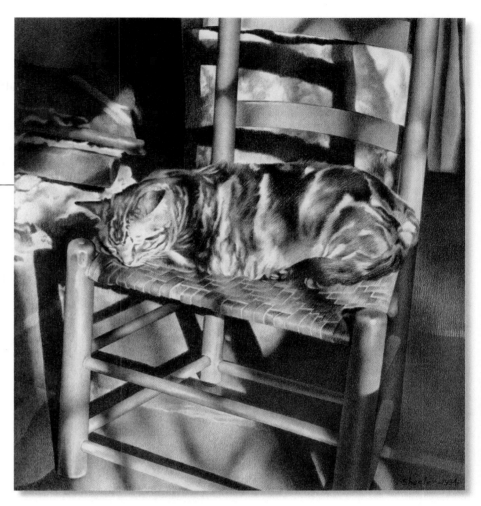

Charles Sheeler. *Feline Felicity,* 1934. Conte crayon on white paper, 21 ¾ by 17 ¾ inches. The Fogg Art Museum, Harvard University, Cambridge, Massachussetts. Purchase of Louise E. Bettens Fund.

Value and Shading

A gradual change from light to dark values is called **shading.** Artists use four basic shading techniques to show form and depth.

Notice the illustrations on page 40 of the four shading techniques most often used by artists. **Blending** is the smooth, gradual change in value. **Stippling** uses a series of dots to create value and shading. **Hatching** is the use of thin parallel lines close together, and **cross-hatching** uses lines that cross each other. Which of these techniques can you identify in the drawing by Charles Sheeler (1883–1965)?

Sketchbook Journal

Sketch a simple object several times, experimenting with each shading technique. Try a variety of drawing media with each technique. Make notes about which media work best for which techniques, and which techniques and media you prefer.

Studio 6 Setup
Contrasting *Values*

Chuck Close. *Emily/Fingerprint,* 1986. Direct gravure etching, 54 ⅛ by 40 ⅜ inches. Edition of 45. Published by Pace Editions, New York.

What technique did Close use to show value?

The difference between light values and dark values in an artwork is called **contrast.** A black area placed next to a white area is an example of high contrast. A light gray area next to a medium gray area is an example of low contrast. Notice these details in the artwork by American artist Chuck Close (1940–):

• The dark values of the subject's hair and the lighter values of gray in the face create high contrast.

• The darker shades of gray around the eyes make those areas appear to recede. The lighter values on the subject's cheeks, nose, and clothing seem to project, adding to the illusion of form.

Stippling on a Large Scale

Chuck Close is known for his large portraits. In an artwork this large, what tool might you use to create stippling? Close used his finger! He dipped his fingertip into powdered graphite or carbon and applied dots using the stippling technique to create form, depth, and contrast. Where do you think Close applied the most fingerprints?

Close's subjects often include his family, friends, himself, and fellow artists. He begins by drawing a grid on a photograph of his subject. Then he begins applying dots of color or values of gray.

Technique Tip

Fingerprint Stippling
Practice using your fingertip to create value and shading. Using a black chalk pastel or charcoal, mark heavily and repeatedly on newsprint to create small "pools" of color. Practice creating different values by varying the space between marks or dots. The closer the dots, the darker the value will be.

Draw a Portrait with Stippling

Use what you have learned about stippling to draw a portrait of yourself or another person.

Materials

✓ 12" × 18" white drawing paper
✓ black and gray chalk pastels
✓ pencil
✓ eraser
✓ black-and-white portrait photograph

1 Using a photograph as a guide, lightly sketch your subject's face onto white drawing paper, filling the page.

2 Use fingerprint stippling to apply medium and dark values to your drawing.

3 Create lighter values by leaving areas white or by erasing dots of chalk with the pencil eraser.

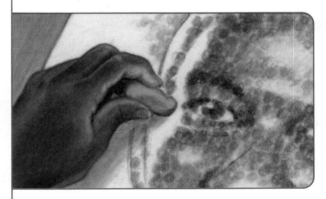

Review and Reflect

- Describe the values and shading you used.
- Where are the darkest and lightest values? Where did you include areas of greatest and least contrast?
- What do you notice about the person for the first time?
- What do you like best about the portrait? Why?

Color

Color is the visual quality of objects created by the amount of light they reflect or absorb. A green object, for example, absorbs all colors of light except green. The green you see is the part of the light that is reflected back to your eyes. Sir Isaac Newton was the first to understand the nature of color. He was also first to discover that white is made up of all the colors of the rainbow.

Colors, also called **hues,** are classified as primary, secondary, or intermediate. **Primary colors** consist of yellow, blue, and red. They cannot be made by mixing other colors. These three colors, along with black and white, can be mixed to make any color you can imagine.

The **secondary colors** are orange, violet, and green, and are made by mixing two primary colors. Mixing yellow and red makes orange, blue and red make violet, and green is mixed from yellow and blue.

Intermediate colors are made by mixing a primary color and a secondary color that are next to each other on the color wheel. For example, blue-violet is made by mixing blue and violet. The primary color is always listed first in the names of intermediate colors.

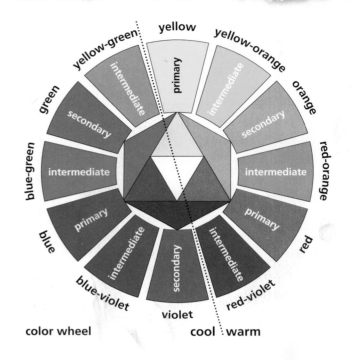

color wheel   cool : warm

Look for primary, secondary, and intermediate colors in nature.

Diana Ong. *Beachcombers,* 1994. Computer graphics. Collection of the artist.

Color and Value

In the last lesson, you read that value is the lightness or darkness of a color. Look at *Beachcombers*, by American artist Diana Ong (1940–). Notice the different values of yellow, blue, and violet. Though it appears to be a painting, Ong created the colors and their values in this artwork using a computer. Colors and their values can express different feelings and moods in an artwork. What mood do the colors in this artwork express?

Research

Discover more about Sir Isaac Newton's experiments with color online or in your local library. How did Newton determine that white light contained the seven colors of the rainbow? Make notes about Newton's discoveries and how you can use his discoveries about color in your artworks.

Warm and Cool *Colors*

André Derain. *Bridge Over the Riou*, 1906. Oil on canvas, 32 ½ by 40 inches. The Museum of Modern Art, NY.

How would you describe the colors in this artwork?

Another way to classify colors is to group them into warm colors and cool colors. Reds, yellows, and oranges are **warm colors.** Greens, blues, and violets are **cool colors.** Look closely at the colors that French artist André Derain (1880–1954) used in *Bridge over the Riou.*

- The bright, warm colors and values of red, yellow, and orange seem to project. The lighter color values give the impression of sunlight.
- The cool, darker blues, violets, and greens add contrast and seem to recede, giving the illusion of depth.

Colors and Feelings

Think about the feelings or moods that warm colors and cool colors express. Warm colors often remind viewers of sunlight, firelight, and the feelings of warmth they convey. Cool colors often express a peaceful and relaxed feeling, but cool colors also may suggest fear or loneliness. Consider the moods and feelings you wish to express as you select colors for your artworks.

Technique Tip

Mixing Paints
When mixing colors, add small amounts of color to get just the color you are looking for. Make adjustments as needed in the amount of paint you mix. To help achieve a violet hue, try mixing a small amount of white paint to the red and blue.

Studio 7

Paint Warm or Cool Colors

Use what you have learned about color to paint an outdoor scene.

Materials

- ✓ color wheel shown on page 44
- ✓ 12" × 18" white paper
- ✓ pencil
- ✓ tempera or acrylic paints
- ✓ mixing containers or trays
- ✓ paintbrushes

1 From the color wheel, choose your favorite warm *and* cool colors. Practice mixing paints to make the colors you have selected.

2 Use a pencil to draw an outdoor scene.

3 Paint the scene. Use the warm or cool colors to fill your paper. Use color to show value, space, and depth.

Review and Reflect

- Describe the colors in your painting.
- Which colors seem to come forward? Which ones seem to recede?
- What mood do the colors of your painting convey?
- Would you like to visit the scene that you painted? Explain.

Lesson 8

Color Schemes

A **color scheme** is a plan for using colors in an artwork. Planning a color scheme in advance helps an artist create the effects he or she wants to achieve.

A **monochromatic** color scheme uses different values of a single hue. This type of color scheme creates a sense of wholeness, or unity.

An **analogous** color scheme uses colors that are side by side on the color wheel and that share a hue. Look at the analogous color scheme on this page. What hue do all the colors share? An analogous color scheme may include both warm and cool colors.

A **complementary** color scheme uses hues that are across from each other on the color wheel; for example, green and red or orange and blue. A complementary color scheme creates a bold, attention-getting artwork.

Neutral color schemes include black, white, and values of gray. Brown is also considered a neutral color by many artists.

monochromatic

analogous

complementary

neutral

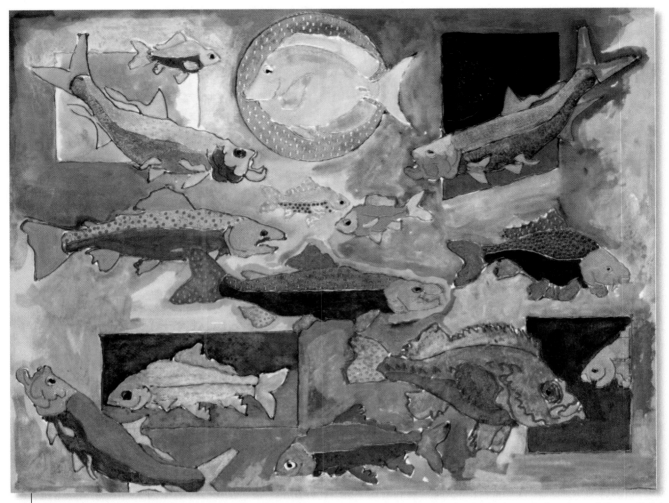

Marilee Whitehouse-Holm. *Fish Scents,* 1996. Watercolor on paper, 22 ½ by 30 inches. Collection of the artist.

Color Schemes and Mood

Notice the colors in this artwork by American artist Marilee Whitehouse-Holm (1949–). She used a complementary color scheme of blues and oranges. The different values of the hues help show space and depth. Notice how the artist's use of neutral colors adds contrast to the brighter hues. Think about the effects the artist wanted to achieve. What feeling or mood does the artwork express? How do the colors contribute to this mood? Think about other color schemes that could be used in a painting of fish.

Visual Culture

You probably use color to choose the clothes you wear each day. Look at the clothing on mannequins in store windows. The clothing is often selected based on its color. Make notes about other locations in your environment where colors are used to attract your attention and tell how.

49

Vincent van Gogh. *Still Life: Vase with Twelve Sunflowers,* 1888. Oil on canvas, 35 ½ by 28 inches. Bavaria State Collection of Paintings, Munich.

What kind of color scheme did Van Gogh use in this painting?

This painting by Vincent van Gogh (1853–1890) shows a monochromatic color scheme. Notice how the yellows give the viewer a feeling of warmth and comfort. The artist got the same feelings from the different values of the warm hue. Van Gogh's use of yellows brought him happiness and joy. Look closely for these details:

- The contrast between the light and dark hues creates implied lines.
- Van Gogh's use of value gives the illusion of form to the vase and flowers.

Properties of Color

You have read that value is one of the properties of color. By changing the value of a hue, an artist can create many variations. Lighter values of a hue, called **tints,** are made by mixing a hue with white. Mixing black with a hue creates a **shade;** it has a darker value than the hue.

Another property of color is **intensity,** or a hue's brightness or dullness. A color in its purest form has the highest intensity. The intensity of a color can be lowered by mixing it with its opposite on the color wheel.

Technique Tip

Clean Water

To be sure your colors stay true and pure, keep clean water handy. Rinsing your brush in the same water over and over can affect the colors you mix. Dirty water can cause your colors to become muddy, or even change the color altogether. Once you rinse your brush, it is also a good idea to blot it well with a paper towel.

Studio 8

Paint in Color Schemes

Use what you have learned about color schemes and color properties to paint a monochromatic scene.

Materials

- ✓ 12" × 18" white paper
- ✓ pencil
- ✓ tempera or acrylic paints
- ✓ paintbrushes
- ✓ mixing containers or trays

1 Develop a monochromatic color scheme for a painting. Mix the tints, shades, and intensities of one hue that you will use.

2 Draw a scene or group of objects for your color scheme. Think about the mood your color scheme will express.

3 Paint the scene using your color scheme.

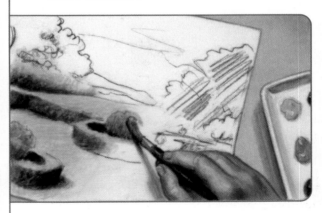

Review and Reflect

- Describe your color scheme.
- How did you show contrast? Where did you use tints and shades?
- What mood or feeling is expressed by your color scheme?
- What do you like best about the color scheme you used?

Texture

Texture is how something feels to the touch or how it appears that it might feel. The way a surface feels is called **tactile texture,** or actual texture. Sandpaper, for example, feels rough. The way a surface appears to your eye is called **visual texture,** or simulated texture, such as shiny or dull. A painting of a silver vase might show both its smooth and shiny textures.

Locate the different visual textures in the painting on this page by Flemish painter Jan van Eyck (ca. 1395–1441). Notice how the chandelier and the mirror on the back wall appear smooth and shiny. How might it feel to touch the frame of the mirror? The artist's use of value helps give the appearance of softness to the figures' clothing. Describe other visual textures you see in the painting.

Jan van Eyck. *Arnolfini Marriage,* 1434. Oil on wood, 32¼ by 23 ½ inches. The National Gallery, London.

How would you describe this texture?

Notice the smooth texture of the rocks.

Texture and Expression

Look at the variety of textures in this sculpture by American artist Deborah Butterfield (1949–). Butterfield used a combination of recycled metal, wood, and even a tire. Notice how these materials help define the form of the horse. Imagine the textures you might feel if you could touch this sculpture. Find rough, smooth, and bumpy textures. Think about why Butterfield chose the materials she did and what she wanted to express about the horse.

Imagine how this sculpture might be different if the artist had used materials such as smooth, finished wood and shiny, polished metals. How would these materials and textures change the meaning of the artwork?

Sketchbook Journal

Record interesting textures by making rubbings with charcoal or crayon and paper. Make sketches of the same objects in your Sketchbook Journal, using shading techniques to show textures. Label the textures with descriptive words.

Lucas Samaras. *Untitled,* 1965. Mixed media, 16 ½ by 14 inches. Newark Museum, Newark, NJ.

Point out rough, smooth, and shiny textures.

Artists use texture to express ideas and feelings, and to add interest to their artworks. They choose materials that have interesting textures and that viewers will respond to in a certain way. Look for these details in this artwork by Lucas Samaras (1936–):

- The reflections of the pointed tacks add visual interest and a sense of motion.
- The rows of yarn add color and interest while providing a bumpy texture.
- The artist's use of mirrors provides visual texture.

Choosing Materials

Samaras combined a variety of materials to create both tactile and visual textures in this box construction. His use of materials also adds a sense of whimsy, or fantasy. Notice how the mirrors create repeated lines and geometric shapes. Where do you notice negative space? Imagine how different materials would change the message and feeling of the artwork. What materials could you use to show tactile and visual texture in your artworks?

Technique Tip

Found Objects

A found object is something one finds, such as spools, toys, and wood, that was not originally intended as part of an artwork. Collect usable found objects that have interesting textures. Look for found objects on your way to school or on a walk. Be sure any objects you collect are free of sharp edges.

Studio 9

Create a Box Construction

Use what you have learned about tactile texture to make a three-dimensional artwork.

Materials

- ✓ sturdy cardboard shoebox with lid
- ✓ found objects
- ✓ photographs or magazine pictures
- ✓ scissors Ⓢ
- ✓ glue
- ✓ tempera or acrylic paints
- ✓ paintbrushes

1 Collect several found objects that reflect your personality or a hobby. Choose objects that have interesting textures.

2 Paint the box and lid, using your favorite colors. Consider gluing photographs or magazine pictures to the box.

3 Arrange the found objects in the box and glue them in place. You may also glue objects to the outside of the box.

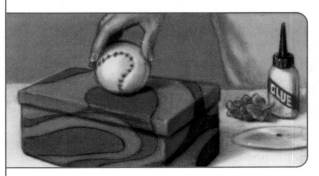

Review and Reflect

- Describe the textures of the objects in your box.
- What do the objects and textures you used add to your box construction?
- How does your box construction reflect your personality? What does it say about you?
- What would you change about your artwork? Why?

Portfolio *Project*

Show Shapes in Motion

Diana Ong. *Angels #2,*
Computer graphics.
Collection of the artist.

Plan

As you have read, artists often use the elements of art to show motion and energy in their artworks. Although it appears to be painted or drawn with oil pastels, Chinese American artist Diana Ong (1940–) created this artwork using a computer. It shows how the artist used lines, shapes, and colors to show a sense of movement. The vibrant colors give a feeling of energy, adding to the action and movement of the flowing shapes.

- The artist's use of color and organic and geometric shapes help create actual and implied lines.
- Ong used tints and shades of blue. How would the mood be different if the artist had used only colors of blue?

Sketchbook Journal

Practice sketching organic and geometric shapes that show motion. Think about how repeating shapes in an artwork can add the illusion of movement. Draw a shape that represents movement. Repeat the shape, allowing some to overlap. What colors will help add a sense of motion?

Materials

- ✓ pencil
- ✓ 9" × 12" tagboard
- ✓ scissors or utility knife ⚠
- ✓ 12" × 18" construction paper
- ✓ chalk or oil pastels

Create

1 In the center of the tagboard, draw one organic or one geometric shape that suggests movement or direction. Then cut out the shape.

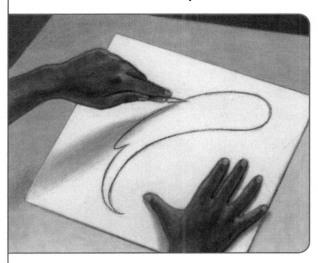

2 Choose a color of construction paper for your background and a few chalk or oil pastels in colors that will blend well.

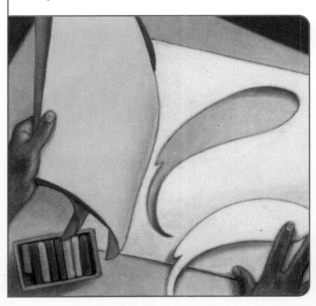

3 Decide in which direction the shapes will move across the background.

4 Use pastels to stencil the shapes onto the background, using both your positive and negative shape cut-outs. Add interest by overlapping some of the shapes.

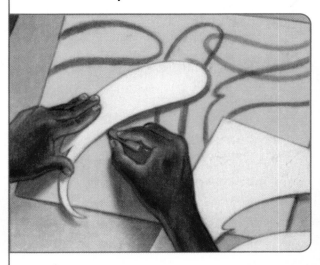

Reflect

- Describe the shapes and colors in your artwork.
- How do the shapes and colors work together to show motion?
- What type of music would best reflect the motion in your artwork? Why?
- What do you like best about your artwork? Explain.

Unit 1 *Review*

Vocabulary Review

A Match each art term below with its definition.

> line   form
> value   geometric shape
> texture   organic shape
> color   space
> neutral   secondary color

1. path left by a dot moving across a surface
2. precise mathematical shape
3. irregular and uneven shape
4. an object with three dimensions
5. describes empty or full areas of an artwork
6. lightness or darkness of a color
7. caused by the amount of light reflected or absorbed by an object
8. made by mixing two primary colors
9. color scheme of black, white, and grays
10. how something feels to the touch

Artists and Their Art

B Each artwork listed in the box appears in this unit. Use the titles to finish the sentences.

> *Mona Lisa*
> *Emily/Fingerprint*
> *Yosemite Falls*
> *The Scream*
> *City Park*
> *Going West*

1. Edvard Munch used line to show sound in ___.
2. ___, by Leonardo, is one of the most famous portraits in history.
3. Thomas Hart Benton used line to show movement in ___.
4. ___, by Albert Bierstadt, is an example of atmospheric perspective.
5. Chuck Close used stippling to create a range of values in ___.
6. Anna Belle Lee Washington used overlapping to show depth in ___.

Thomas Hart Benton

Chuck Close

Respond to Art

C Look at André Derain's painting of *Charing Cross Bridge, London.* In a class discussion or on a sheet of paper, match each art term below with examples from the painting.

André Derain. *Charing Cross Bridge, London*, 1906.
Oil on canvas, 31 ⅝ by 39 ½ inches. National Gallery
of Art, Washington, D.C.

Art Terms

1. foreground
2. background
3. complementary colors
4. texture
5. implied lines
6. stippling
7. negative space
8. overlapping

Unit 1 *Review*

Write About Art

Descriptive Paragraph

D Look back at the artworks in this unit. Choose one to describe in a paragraph. Copy the chart below and fill in the seven elements of art in the first column. In the second column, write details about how the artist used each element. Use the completed chart to help you organize your paragraph.

Name of Artwork

Elements of Art Used	Descriptive Details
1.	
2.	
3.	
4.	
5.	
6.	
7.	

Your Studio Work

E Answer these questions in your Sketchbook Journal or on a separate sheet of paper.

1. What skill or technique in this unit interested you or challenged you the most? Explain.
2. What problems did you have as you worked with new skills and techniques? How did you solve them? What will you do differently next time?
3. Which artworks inspired your own art-making process?
4. Choose one artwork to keep in your portfolio. Tell why you chose it.

Put It All Together

David Hockney. *Double Entrance*, 1993–1995. Oil on canvas, 72 by 168 inches. Smithsonian American Art Museum, Washington, D.C.

F **Discuss or write about Hockney's painting *Double Entrance,* using the four steps for critically viewing artwork.**

1. **Describe** Describe the lines and shapes you see. What might the shapes represent?
2. **Analyze** How did Hockney use the elements of art to show this outdoor scene? Write several words about how each element of art listed below is used in *Double Entrance*.

color	shape	value
texture	space	form

3. **Interpret** What do you think is the message of this artwork? What is the mood? What does it suggest about the artist's feelings about the California landscape?
4. **Judge** British artist David Hockney (1937–) lives in California. The Los Angeles lifestyle and landscape are important parts of his artworks. Was Hockney successful in conveying the California landscape in this artwork? Explain.

"The moment you cheat for the sake of beauty, you know you're an artist."

—DAVID HOCKNEY

Minnie Evans. *King,* 1962. North Carolina Museum of Art.

Unit 2

The Principles of Design

In Unit 1, you learned about the elements of art, the basic parts and symbols that make up artworks. This unit will help you discover the principles of design, the guides used by artists in arranging the elements of art and planning visual compositions. The seven **principles of design** include **balance, emphasis, proportion, rhythm, pattern, unity,** and **variety.**

These principles will help guide your understanding and appreciation of works of art. They will also provide a common vocabulary for discussing visual art. You will discover how artists use the principles of design in their artworks, and you will have opportunities to experiment with them in your own works of art.

This painting by American artist Minnie Evans (1892–1987) shows the artist's use of the principles of balance, pattern, unity, and variety. With no formal art instruction, Evans developed a highly personal and expressive style of art using the principles of design.

About *the Artist*

Born in a log cabin in North Carolina, **Minnie Evans** began making art in her forties. She used vibrant colors to represent her dreams and visions, often the subjects of her paintings. Read more about Minnie Evans on page 84.

Balance

How would you describe each side of the sculpture below? You might say the two sides are equal or balanced. **Balance** is achieved when the elements are arranged to give the appearance of overall equality or stability in an artwork. In **symmetrical balance,** also called formal balance, the two halves nearly mirror each other. In **radial balance,** elements spread out from a center point. A starfish is an example of radial balance.

In what other natural objects might you see radial balance?

Artist unknown, Mayan. *Urn or Brazier in the Shape of a Priest,* Pre-Columbian.

Gustave Caillebotte. *Paris Street, Rainy Day,* 1877. Oil on canvas, 83 ½ by 108 ¾ inches. The Art Institute of Chicago, Chicago, IL.

Asymmetrical Balance

Why does this artwork appear balanced? French artist Gustave Caillebotte (1848–1894) used **asymmetrical balance,** or the application of equal visual weight, in this painting. The two sides of the artwork are not the same, yet the visual weight, or use of elements to draw the viewer's attention, are nearly equal.

Artists create asymmetrical balance, also known as informal balance, using color, line, shape, and other elements. For example, a large shape on the right might balance a small patch of bright color on the left. How did Caillebotte balance the couple in the foreground?

Sketchbook Journal

Nature loves balance. Look for examples of symmetrical, radial, and asymmetrical balance in the natural environment. Draw and label at least two examples of each kind of balance. Make notes about where you found each example and what attracted your attention to it.

Studio 1 Setup
Balance *in Three Dimensions*

Artist unknown. *Eskimo Mask.* Boulogne Museum, Boulogne-sur-Mer, France.

What types of balance did the artist use in this mask?

Artists create balance in three-dimensional works of art as well as in paintings and drawings. The artist of this mask chose to include several kinds of balance. Look for these details:

- The mask as a whole shows symmetrical balance, although the two sides are not exact mirror images. Shapes are repeated on either side of the mask.

- The patterns within each circular disk around the "face" create radial balance. The artist's use of color adds to the mask's overall balance.

Balance and Expression

Symmetrical balance can often evoke a feeling of order and calmness. Asymmetrical balance sometimes reflects feelings of tension or instability. Think about how the artist's use of symmetrical balance affects your response to the mask. What mood does it express? How do the shapes and colors contribute to this mood? Consider how you might use balance to express a particular mood or feeling in your artworks.

Technique Tip

Working with Cardboard
Avoid unwanted creases when shaping corrugated cardboard. Try wrapping it around an object similar to the shape you want to achieve. Be sure to wrap it with the channels rather than against them. To help the cardboard hold its shape, use several strips of masking tape on the back. The tape can then be removed once you've completed the project.

66

Make a Mask with Balance

Use what you have learned about balance to make a mask that represents a special occasion, culture, or event.

Materials

✓ 8" × 10" piece of corrugated cardboard, with channels running 10 inches vertically
✓ pencil
✓ hole punch
✓ tempera paints and brushes
✓ construction paper
✓ scissors ⚠
✓ glue
✓ yarn, feathers, pipe cleaners, beads and other decorations
✓ elastic or rubber band

1 Bend the cardboard into an arc. Use a pencil to mark the location of the eyes and nose, and punch holes for them.

2 Paint a face on the mask. As the paint is drying, use construction paper to create a three-dimensional nose and glue it on.

3 Adorn your mask and create balance by gluing on other decorations. Punch holes and add elastic so you can wear the mask.

Review and Reflect

- Describe the shapes and colors in your mask.
- What kind of balance did you show? What parts of your mask help create balance?
- What feeling or mood does your mask express?
- What do you like best about your mask? Where might you wear it? Why?

Lesson 2

Emphasis

Mary Cassatt.
Motherhood, 1897.
Pastel on paper,
21 ½ by 18 inches.
Musée d'Orsay,
Paris, France.

When you circle a word in a sentence or whistle and clap at a thrilling point in a football game, you are adding emphasis. **Emphasis** in artworks is the importance artists add to certain objects or areas to attract the viewer's attention. This attention-getting object or area is often the focal point, or center of interest in the artwork.

An artist may make a certain object the focal point of an artwork by placing it in the center or by making it the largest element. What is the focal point of *Motherhood* by American artist Mary Cassatt (1844–1926)?

Artists also often create emphasis through **dominance,** or making one element more noticeable than others. For example, in a composition made up of many geometric shapes, the artist may add more triangles than squares or circles. The triangles have dominance in the composition.

Contrast is yet another method of creating emphasis. You have read that contrast can be shown using light and dark values. An object painted in colors of very different intensities can also show contrast and emphasis.

Look again at *Motherhood.* In what other ways did Cassatt emphasize the child? What techniques did she use to do this?

Andrew Wyeth. *The Chambered Nautilus,* 1956. Tempera on panel, 24 3/4 by 48 1/4 inches. Wadsworth Atheneum, Hartford, CT.

Emphasis and Meaning

American artist Andrew Wyeth (1917–) incorporated a variety of techniques to show emphasis in *The Chambered Nautilus.* Notice the object that first catches the viewer's eye. Placed at the center of the artwork and painted in a bright, contrasting color, the window becomes the main focal point.

Notice how the light from the window makes the girl a second focal point. What other object is emphasized? How? What meaning do you think the artist intended?

Cassatt and Wyeth both used color to show emphasis in these artworks, yet their color palettes are very different. How does each artist's use of color affect emphasis and meaning in these artworks?

Sketchbook Journal

Make sketches of three or four simple objects of varying sizes, such as a shoe, a chair, and a plant. Select one part of each object to enlarge or relocate to show emphasis. Make notes indicating the techniques you used. Describe how you can apply these techniques to your artworks.

Emphasis *with Color*

Gil Mayers. *Time Piece.* Mixed media, 16 by 16 inches. Gilbert Mayers.

What parts of the artwork did the artist emphasize?

The elements of color and shape play a major role in this painting. American artist Gil Mayers (1947–) used these and other elements to emphasize objects and create a mood. Notice these details:

- The bright, violet instrument is the focal point of the artwork. Color, contrast, and balance direct your eye to the instrument.
- The lines and shapes of the other instruments and the figures draw your eye to the center of the painting.
- The contrast and intensities of the various colors emphasize the larger instrument.

Emphasis and Mood

The parts of an artwork that an artist emphasizes and the techniques the artist uses often affect the mood of the artwork.

In *Time Piece,* Mayers chose to emphasize the violet instrument. What mood do the colors and shapes create? What kind of music do you think these instruments are playing?

Technique Tip

Contrast in Emphasis

Contrast can help create emphasis. Practice creating contrast by dividing a sheet of paper into four sections. Fill each section with two contrasting colors. Determine which color combinations work best or how you might change them to create emphasis in your artworks.

Design a Product Package

Use what you have learned about emphasis to design packaging for a breakfast cereal.

Materials

- ✓ empty cereal box
- ✓ 12" × 18" white drawing paper
- ✓ ruler
- ✓ pencil
- ✓ tempera paint
- ✓ brushes
- ✓ water container
- ✓ paper towels
- ✓ scissors ⚠
- ✓ glue

1 Research and create a new cereal and give it a name. Measure the front of the cereal box and draw its dimensions on drawing paper.

2 Draw your design for the front of the box. Use what you have learned about emphasis to make the cereal attractive to viewers.

3 Choose colors that help show emphasis; then paint your design. Cut it out and glue it to the empty cereal box.

Review and Reflect

- Describe the elements of art you used to show emphasis.
- What objects did you emphasize, and what techniques did you use?
- What does your cereal box design say about the cereal product?
- Do you think consumers would buy your new cereal? Why or why not?

Proportion

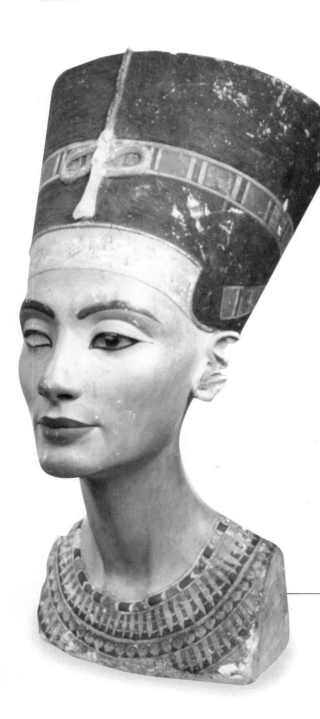

When you buy clothes, you buy them in a size that fits you, or in proportion to your body size. **Proportion** is a principle of design that refers to how two elements relate to one another in size.

Artists often use the human body as a standard of proportion. For example, you are huge compared to an ant but tiny compared to a mountain. Look at the ancient Egyptian sculpture of Queen Nefertiti. It shows standard proportion. The artist of this ancient work made each facial feature in proportion to the others, giving the sculpture a realistic appearance.

This portrait bust of the queen was found among the ruins at Tell el-Amarna. Nefertiti reigned during the Amarna period of ancient Egypt. In artworks of this period she is often shown the same size as her pharaoh husband, Akhenaten. She is also notably portrayed at his side in ancient relief sculptures. What do you think this says about their relationship? How would this sculpture be different if the artist had chosen to change the proportions?

Artist unknown. *Nefertiti,* ca. 1365 B.C. Painted limestone, height 19 ⅝ inches. Bode Museum, Berlin, Germany.

Edward Hicks. *The Peaceable Kingdom,* ca. 1840–1845. Oil on canvas, 18 by 24 ⅛ inches. Brooklyn Museum of Art, Dick S. Ramsay Fund. 40.340.

Size and Placement

What do you notice about the animals and people in this painting? Painted by American artist Edward Hicks (1780–1849), the artwork shows how artists use size and placement to make a statement or convey a mood. The size relationships between the animals and people do not follow standard proportions. Instead, Hicks made some of the animals much larger than normal. Notice also where the larger animals are in relation to the people and other objects. What message do you think Hicks wanted to convey?

Research

Learn more about how the ancient Egyptians used proportion in their artworks. Visit your local library or do an Internet search. Use key search phrases such as *ancient Egyptian art*. You can also visit online museums such as the Metropolitan Museum of Art in New York City. Make notes about the results of your findings.

Jacob Lawrence. *Harriet Tubman Series No. 7,* 1939–1940. Casein tempera on gessoed hardboard, 17 7/8 by 12 inches. Collection of Hampton University Museum, Hampton, VA.

What do you notice about the proportions in this artwork?

Proportion and Scale

As an important aspect of proportion, **scale** is used to measure objects against a common standard. An object of miniature or small scale might be a doll or toy truck. The Statue of Liberty is an example of monumental or larger-than-life scale. Imagine how you might use proportion, scale, size, and placement in your artworks.

By changing or altering the size relationships of objects, artists create **altered proportion.** American artist Jacob Lawrence (1917–2000) altered the proportions in his representation of Harriet Tubman. As an escaped slave, Tubman became part of the Underground Railroad, an organization that helped other enslaved people escape to the North. Look for these examples of altered proportion in Lawrence's depiction of Tubman:

- The figure's arms and hands are exaggerated in size.
- The striking power of the forearms depicts her strength.

Technique Tip

Observing Proportion

Look around you to get a sense of how artists alter proportions. The editorial page of your local newspaper is a good place to start. This page often includes editorial or political cartoons in which the artist has altered the figure's proportion. Notice the features that have been altered. Consider why the artist might have chosen to alter that feature.

Studio 3

Paint a Portrait

Use what you have learned to paint a picture of a person, altering proportions to show emphasis.

Materials

✓ pencil and eraser
✓ white drawing paper
✓ large sheet of painting paper or board
✓ tempera paints
✓ brushes
✓ water container
✓ paper towels

1 Use a pencil and drawing paper to draw a person performing an activity. Alter the person's proportions to create emphasis.

2 Redraw the sketch on painting paper. Use simple lines, and refine the proportions to get them just as you want them.

3 Use the sketch as a guide for your painting. Use strong, simple colors to create additional emphasis.

Review and Reflect

- Describe the person in your painting and the activity he or she is performing.
- How did you choose which proportions to alter? Do the colors and altered proportions create emphasis?
- What did you intend the altered proportion to express about the person or activity?
- What title would you give your artwork? Why?

Rhythm

Just like music, art has rhythm. **Rhythm** in art uses repeated elements to express a sense of visual or actual movement. Repeating the same element, such as a shape, creates **regular rhythm.** Two or more elements repeated on an alternating basis create **alternating rhythm.** To create **progressive rhythm,** a repeated element is changed in progression. For example, a shape may get larger each time it is repeated.

Look at the elements Chinese American artist Diana Ong (1940–) used to create alternating rhythm. The repeated symbols of the Statue of Liberty create a checkerboard effect. These elements also create a sense of movement. You might feel like your eyes are dancing around the composition. What other elements add to the sense of rhythm and movement?

Types of Rhythm

regular rhythm

alternating rhythm

progressive rhythm

Diana Ong. *Miss Liberty III (Orange).* Computer Original, © Diana Ong.

What type of rhythm does this artwork show?

Victor Vasarely. *Vega-Nor,*
1969. Oil on canvas,
78 3/4 by 78 3/4 inches.
Albright-Knox Art Gallery,
Buffalo, NY.

Rhythm and Motion

Do you get a sense of motion or movement when you look at this painting? Hungarian artist Victor Vasarely (1908–1997) used progressive rhythm to make the center appear to be moving toward the viewer. Notice how Vasarely repeated lines and shapes, but each element changes each time it repeats. Lines become thicker and farther apart toward the center of the artwork. The squares become larger with curved sides, adding to the illusion of forward motion. Vasarely combined his knowledge of math, science, and the elements of art to trick the eye in his paintings. Look again at the center vertical and horizontal lines in *Vega-Nor.* Although they seem to curve, they are actually straight. How do the colors add to the visual rhythm?

Sketchbook Journal

Look for examples of each kind of visual rhythm in your environment. Draw and label examples of both natural and human-made objects and scenes that show visual rhythm. How might you use these objects and scenes in your artworks?

77

Hale Woodruff. *Georgia Landscape,* ca. 1934–1935. Oil on canvas, 21 ⅛ by 25 ⅝ inches. Smithsonian American Art Museum, Washington, D.C.

What elements help create visual rhythm in this artwork?

Musical rhythm is made up of beats. Musicians create different rhythms by varying the timing and volume of sounds. Using the elements of art and the principles of design, artists can suggest a musical sense with visual rhythm. Look at this painting by American artist Hale Woodruff (1900–1980). Notice these details as you think about what kind of musical rhythm it might represent:

- The lines and shapes suggest a flowing smoothness of rhythm.
- The flowing lines and shapes tend to lead the viewer's eye in a back and forth motion through the artwork.
- The colors become brighter and more intense toward the center of the artwork.

Musical Rhythm in Artworks

An artist may listen to music and create an artwork that expresses its rhythm visually. In fact, using musical rhythm as a model is a good way to experiment with creating visual rhythm.

Technique Tip

Lines with Rhythm

Load your brush differently for different lines. Short lines require less paint than longer lines, so load your brush accordingly. Begin with a gentle touch and increase pressure gradually. Practice to achieve the results you want.

Studio 4

Paint a Landscape to Music

Use what you have learned about rhythm to paint an outdoor scene that expresses musical rhythm.

Materials

- ✓ musical selection
- ✓ pencil
- ✓ large sheet of painting paper or board
- ✓ tempera paints
- ✓ brushes
- ✓ water container
- ✓ paper towels

1 While listening to a musical selection, imagine an interesting outdoor scene. Listen closely to the music's rhythm.

2 Use a pencil to draw the scene, using lines and shapes that express the rhythm and mood of the music.

3 Use tempera to paint the scene. Paint with short and long strokes to express the rhythm of the music.

Review and Reflect

- Describe the scene in your painting.
- How do the colors and lines in your scene reflect the rhythm of the music?
- What is the mood or feeling of your painting?
- Could your scene also reflect the rhythm of a different musical selection? Explain.

Lesson 5

Pattern

Patterns are everywhere. How many patterns can you see around you right now? In art, **pattern** is simply the regular repetition of a line, shape, or color. While rhythm conveys a sense of motion, and may use a pattern to do so, patterns themselves may or may not show motion. Learning about pattern and its relationship with rhythm will help you discover patterns in the natural and human-made environments.

Artist unknown, Chinese, Yang-Shao Culture. *Storage Jar,* 2500 B.C. Clay, height 14 ½ inches. The Lowe Art Museum, The University of Miami, Florida.

How did the maker of this jar create both rhythm and pattern?

Rhythm and pattern also appear in nature such as on this zebra.

Philip Taaffe. *North African Strip*, 1993. Mixed media on canvas, 113 ½ by 89 inches. Gagosian Gallery, New York.

Patterns in the Environment

Patterns can be created using actual or implied lines, colors, shapes, and textures. They appear in the limbs of trees and in the feathers of birds. They may be simple or extremely complex. This artwork by American artist Philip Taaffe (1955–) includes complex patterns made with stencils.

The artwork's title provides a clue to the artist's inspiration. Taaffe borrowed patterns seen in metal-and-glass lanterns made in North Africa. What elements and objects did Taaffe repeat to create patterns? Are patterns found in the natural environment different from those in the human-made environment? Explain.

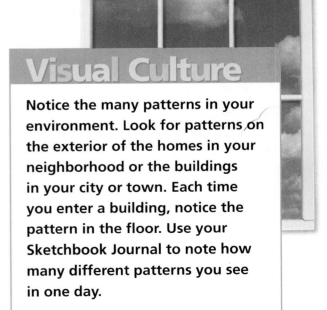

Visual Culture

Notice the many patterns in your environment. Look for patterns on the exterior of the homes in your neighborhood or the buildings in your city or town. Each time you enter a building, notice the pattern in the floor. Use your Sketchbook Journal to note how many different patterns you see in one day.

Artist unknown, Persian. *Panel of mosaic tilework,* 14th or 15th century. Earthenware and colored enamels. Victoria and Albert Museum, London, England.

What creates rhythm and pattern in this artwork?

This Persian tilework is more than five hundred years old and is a good example of how artists combine rhythm and pattern to create interest. Notice these details:

- The artist repeated floral patterns. There are three types of flowers set in three distinct patterns.
- The lines of the artwork create rhythm. The repeating curving stems and tendrils of the plant convey a sense of motion.
- The repeated colors create a pattern and emphasize the plant patterns.

Rhythm, Pattern, and Function

Objects that include rhythmic patterns can also be functional, or serve a purpose. Think about patterns you find in your environment. Patterns in floors, for example, add interest to the surfaces people walk on. This tilework represents a panel from a series. Imagine how the entire artwork might appear with the rhythmic pattern of the panel repeated. Think about where and how the larger artwork might have been used. Where might you see similar artworks today?

Technique Tip

Holding Objects in Place

Use masking or other tape to hold items where you want them until the glue dries. Choose a tape that does not leave marks when removed. Give the glue plenty of time to dry.

Studio 5

Eastland

Create a Wall Hanging

Use what you have learned about pattern to make a burlap wall hanging showing rhythm.

Materials

- ✓ 12" × 18" piece of burlap
- ✓ scraps of yarn, thread, fabric
- ✓ scissors ⚠
- ✓ beads and found objects
- ✓ glue
- ✓ two 13-inch long sticks or dowels

1 Pull horizontal threads out of the burlap at regular intervals—but not too near the top or bottom—to make a pattern.

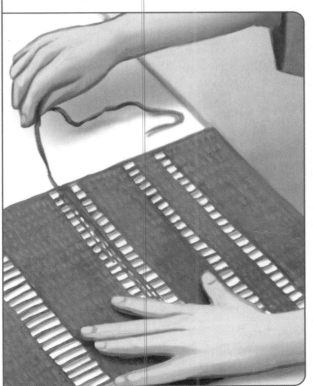

2 Tie short pieces of yarn, thread, or fabric strips to pulled-out areas. Repeat materials and colors to create patterns.

3 Glue or tie beads and found objects to the burlap in a pattern. Glue sticks to top and bottom of burlap for hanging.

Review and Reflect

- Describe patterns in your wall hanging. What elements or objects repeat?
- How do the patterns in your wall hanging show visual rhythm?
- What meaning or mood do the found objects in your wall hanging convey?
- What do you like best about your wall hanging? Why?

Meet *the Artist*

Minnie Evans

Minnie Evans was born in a log cabin in North Carolina in 1892. She went to school for only a few years, and did not begin to make art until she was in her forties. Yet, she became an internationally respected artist whom *Newsweek* magazine described as "breathtakingly gifted."

Minnie Evans has been described as a "beautiful dreamer."

"I have no imagination. I never plan a drawing, they just happen."
—MINNIE EVANS

A Quiet Childhood

Minnie Evans was born into a family that had come to the United States from Trinidad during the slave trade. Evans's grandmother, whom Evans called Mama Mary, was born a slave and freed when she was a girl. Mama Mary and Evans's mother, Ella, brought her up in Wilmington, North Carolina. Evans went to elementary school and then began working. She sold seafood door-to-door and later became a servant.

Visions and Fame

Evans got married when she was sixteen, and she raised three sons. In 1935, she began to draw the visions that she had seen in dreams and daydreams all her life. When she went to work as a gatekeeper at Airlie Gardens, Evans began selling her artwork to visitors. Her work was first shown in Wilmington in 1961 and in New York City in 1966. *Design Made at Airlie Gardens* was accepted by the National Museum of American Art in 1975, the same year that Evans had a solo show at the Whitney Museum of American Art. A documentary film about Evans and her artwork was made in 1983. Evans died in 1987 at the age of ninety-five.

Talk About It

- Why do you think Evans waited so long to begin drawing and painting?

- Look at *King* and *Design Made at Airlie Gardens* on pages 62 and 87. What clues do they give about Evans's visions?

The Life of Minnie Evans

1890

1892
Minnie Jones Evans born in Long Creek, North Carolina

Evans marries Julius Caesar Evans
1908

1915

Evans draws her first two pictures
1935

Airlie Gardens

1940

Evans begins working at Airlie Gardens
1948

Evans's husband dies
1956

First public showing of Evans's artwork in Wilmington, North Carolina
1961

Whitney Museum of American Art

First New York exhibition of Evans's artworks
1966
1965

Solo exhibition of Evans's artworks at Whitney Museum of American Art in New York; National Museum of American Art accepts *Design Made at Airlie Gardens*
1975

Documentary film *The Angel That Stands by Me: Minnie Evans's Art* produced
1983
1987
Evans dies at age 95
1990

Look *and Compare*

Designs from the Mid-Twentieth Century

American artist Minnie Evans (1892–1987) never received formal art training. She left the South only once in her long life. Dutch artist M. C. Escher (1898–1972) studied architecture and art in Holland, and lived in Italy, Switzerland, and Belgium. Yet from these two very different people came equally vibrant, rhythmic, and powerful images.

Evans's Vision

For years, Evans worked as a gatekeeper at Airlie Gardens in North Carolina, where she made this artwork. Although it is not a painting of the gardens, it's not hard to tell how the gardens influenced the artwork. Think about how Evans used the principles of design. You can easily see the symmetrical balance of the artwork. Find several elements that repeat. Which attract your eye the most?

Escher's Vision

Now look at *Circle Limit III* by Escher. Like Evans's painting, Escher's artwork was influenced both by things he had seen and by his imagination. Can you see evidence of the architecture he studied? Notice how the fish become smaller as they progress toward the outer edge. Although this print appears playful, Escher created it with mathematical precision, leaving no space in between the images of the fish. What types of balance did he show?

Though Evans and Escher lived very different lives, they lived during the same time period. Look at the similarities in their artworks. Both works combine observation and imagination, and both works provoke the imagination of the viewer. Both are colorful, symmetrically balanced, and pleasing to the eye, and each sets off thoughts and questions in the viewer's mind.

Both Evans and Escher were influenced by their environments.

Minnie Evans. *Design Made at Airlie Gardens,* 1967. Oil and mixed media on canvas board, 19 ⅞ by 23 ⅞ inches. Smithsonian American Museum, Washington, D.C.

M. C. Escher. *Circle Limit III,* 1959. Woodcut, diameter 16 ⅜ inches. © 2003 Cordon Art B.V., Baarn, Holland. All rights reserved.

Compare & Contrast

- You see similarities in color and imaginative play. What are some ways that the paintings differ?

- Compare these artworks to the tilework on page 82 or the Chinese jar on page 80. What similarities and differences do you see?

Unity

What feeling do you get when viewing *Nataraja* by Bridget Riley? Her combination of repeated shapes and colors might give you a feeling of movement and energy.

Notice how these elements move your eye around the composition. They also provide **unity,** or the sense of belonging together.

Artists achieve unity in many ways. One method is to repeat a color, shape, or other element. Another is to use related colors. As you can see here, artists may use more than one technique to give their artworks unity. In addition to shapes and colors, what other element provides unity in this painting?

Bridget Riley. *Nataraja*, 1993. Oil on canvas, 64 ⅓ by 88 ¾ inches. Tate Gallery, London.

Franz Marc. *The Monkey (Frieze),* 1911. Oil on canvas, 29 ²/₃ by 52 ½ inches. Hamburg Kunsthalle, Hamburg, Germany.

Unity and Expression

Notice the elements that German artist Franz Marc (1880–1916) used to give unity to *The Monkey (Frieze).* He repeated the shapes of the monkeys and combined them with the similarly repeated shapes of the foliage. He also used the monkeys to create a diagonal line, adding the feeling of movement. How did Marc add interest and distinction to the monkeys? What other elements did he use to unify the painting?

A frieze is a horizontal band that is often used around the upper part of a wall. This ornamental decoration was also used in ancient Greek architecture. Pottery and furniture can also include a frieze. Think about why this painting includes the word in its title.

Sketchbook Journal

Find a scene that shows unity. You might choose a garden that has different kinds of flowers in related colors, or a building with many similar lines and angles. Make a sketch of the scene using colored pencils to show unifying colors. Include notes about the elements that emphasize unity.

Unity *Through Details*

Angel Botello. *Las Lavanderas (The Washerwomen),* 20th century. Oil on masonite, 37 ½ by 48 inches. Private collection.

What unifying elements do you see in this artwork?

This painting of washerwomen by Spanish artist Angel Botello (1913–1986) makes use of the elements of color, line, and shape to achieve unity. Look for these unifying details in the painting:

- The shapes of the human forms vary in size and are repeated in the shapes of the laundry.
- The artist used tints and shades of blue throughout the composition. The other colors add interest and draw the viewer's attention to the figures.

Unifying Elements

Remember, one important way to create unity is to repeat elements throughout the artwork. By using unifying elements in their compositions, artists make all of the parts work together as a whole. All of these elements contribute to the grace of Botello's *Las Lavanderas (The Washerwomen).*

Technique Tip

Paint Stamping

Found objects make great stamps. The application of paint to the found objects, however, can make a difference in the desired effects. For example, too much paint may make the stamp appear solid and without texture. Too little paint may prevent the texture of the object from being fully exposed.

Studio 6

Make a Checkerboard

Use what you have learned about unity to make a checkerboard. Include tints, shades, and textures in your design.

Materials

- ✓ 16" × 16" mat board or illustration board
- ✓ pencil
- ✓ ruler
- ✓ acrylic or tempera paints
- ✓ paintbrush
- ✓ found object with texture to use as stamp
- ✓ paper towels

1 Use a pencil and ruler to draw a grid of two-inch squares that cover the whole board.

2 Before you paint, plan a color scheme that will show unity. Then paint every other square in colors of your choice.

3 Brush other colors of paint onto a textured part of a found object. Use it to stamp the unpainted squares.

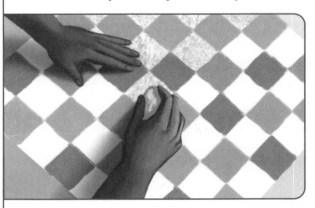

Review and Reflect

- Describe the design of your checkerboard.
- What techniques did you use to create unity?
- What is unique and interesting about your board?
- What did you like best—and least—about making your checkerboard? Why?

Lesson 7

Variety

While unity holds a visual composition together, variety gives it interest and energy. As an art term, **variety** means the combination of elements of art that makes a composition lively and interesting. Did you ever see a photograph of a crowd at a sports event? Among the unity of people, the variety of expressions and colors adds interest to the repeated element of the figures.

Artists may combine organic and geometric shapes, or contrast warm and cool colors. They may show differences among similar objects, as in the sports photograph example. Consider how you might apply the elements of art to create variety in your artworks. You may choose to use a unique combination of shapes and textures. Or, you may want to use a monochromatic color scheme, and then add a splash of excitement with a complementary color!

The variety that exists in nature is often a source of ideas for artworks.

Franz Marc. *A Red Bull,* 1912. © Pushkin Museum of Fine Arts, Moscow, Russia.

Unity and Variety

You have read how artists often repeat elements to create unity. This painting by German artist Franz Marc (1880–1916) is an example of how an artist combines unity and variety in a single work. Notice the elements Marc used to create unity. He repeated rounded shapes in the bull and in the background. He included angular lines and geometric shapes to add interest and variety. While these elements help unify the painting, their differences help create variety. How does the area of white in the center add variety and interest?

Sketchbook Journal

Draw the same animal or object three times. Attempt to create unity and variety in all three sketches. Vary the ways in which you create unity or variety. For example, one sketch may use similar colors to create unity, while another uses differing colors to create variety.

Joseph Cornell. *Box with Objects,* 1941.
Mixed media. Private collection.

How did the artist create variety in this artwork?

American artist Joseph Cornell (1903–1972) is known for his assemblage artworks. An **assemblage** is a collection of found or recycled objects arranged into a unified composition. Look closely to discover how Cornell expressed both unity and variety. Notice these details:

- The assemblage includes a combination of mostly geometric shapes and forms.
- The organic-shaped piece of wood adds variety and repeats the horizontal lines of the frame.
- Circular shapes and forms are repeated in each compartment.

Variety and Theme

Cornell used unusual and common objects in this composition. His use of repeated geometric shapes provides a unifying theme. He created variety by using circular shapes and forms of different materials. Notice how the materials also create variety in tactile and visual textures. Think about some of the objects you may have collected. How could you arrange them to show unity and variety?

Technique Tip

Cardboard Boxes

When using a cardboard box or shoebox in your artworks, it sometimes helps to reinforce the corners and seams. To keep the box firm and help it hold its shape, apply masking tape to the corners and seams. This will prevent these areas from separating or tearing. If you don't like the appearance of the tape, you can either paint it or apply designs with markers.

Studio 7

Make a Fantasy Box

Use what you have learned about variety to make a fantasy box that shows unity and variety.

Materials

- ✓ found objects
- ✓ magazines, scraps of wallpaper and wrapping paper, greeting cards, and maps
- ✓ shoebox lid
- ✓ posterboard or foam core board
- ✓ scissors ⑤
- ✓ white glue
- ✓ markers

1 Choose a theme for your fantasy box. Select images and found objects that express your theme.

2 Arrange your images and objects in the box lid. Use posterboard or foam core board if you want to add compartments or dimension.

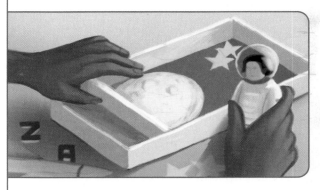

3 Glue your paper scraps, images, and objects in place. Use markers to add details.

Review and Reflect

- Describe the images and objects in your fantasy box.
- How did you create both unity and variety?
- Which image or objects best express your theme? Why do you think so?
- Does your box look like your planning sketches? Explain.

95

Portfolio *Project*

Paint Two Views

Josephine Trotter. *Interior With Garden.* Oil on canvas, 32 by 26 inches. © Josephine Trotter.

Plan

British artist Josephine Trotter (1940–) uses the elements of art to create colorful paintings of indoor and outdoor scenes. She often combines these scenes in one artwork, like the one above. She arranges the elements using the principles of design to express her ideas and feelings about these scenes. Notice these details in her painting above:

- The artwork is asymmetrically balanced by the open door and the window on the right. Trotter used tints and shades to help show space and distance.
- The repeated shapes in the windowpanes and the curtains add pattern and rhythm. How did Trotter show emphasis?
- The artist's use of cool colors provides unity. How did Trotter achieve variety?

Use what you have learned about the principles of design to make a painting with two views. Include a view of both an indoor and outdoor scene in your painting.

Sketchbook Journal

Draw an imagined indoor scene. Use linear perspective to show space and depth. Include objects such as furniture, windows, and at least one door. Then draw an imagined outdoor scene. Consider how you can use the principles of design to combine the two scenes.

Materials

- ✓ magazine photographs (optional)
- ✓ Sketchbook Journal sketch (optional)
- ✓ pencil
- ✓ 12" × 18" watercolor paper
- ✓ tempera paints
- ✓ brushes
- ✓ water jar
- ✓ paper towels
- ✓ crayons

Create

1 Using your Sketchbook Journal sketch or a photograph, draw both an interior and exterior view. Include what you have learned about the elements of art and principles of design in your scene.

2 As you draw, include a focal point and areas of patterns. Add objects that might be seen in both the indoor and outdoor areas of your scene.

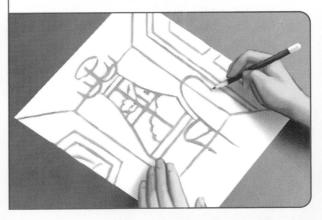

3 Choose colors to paint your indoor and outdoor scene. Consider how your color selections will help you show contrast, value, pattern, rhythm, unity, and variety.

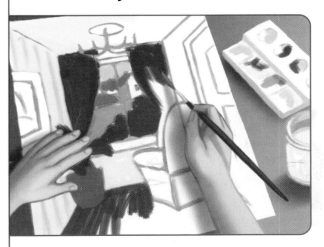

4 Once the paint has dried, use crayons to add details. Enhance the patterns or add texture to certain areas.

Reflect

- What elements of art and principles of design did you include in your scene?
- How did your understanding of the principles of design help you express your ideas?
- What challenges did you face in this activity? How did you solve them?
- Does your scene show a place that viewers might like to visit? Explain.

97

Unit 2 *Review*

Vocabulary Review

A Match each art term below with its definition.

> variety   proportion
> scale   emphasis
> rhythm   assemblage
> pattern   radial balance
> balance   unity

1. an artwork made from a collection of objects
2. an element or object repeated in a regular way
3. the use of differing elements in a single artwork to create interest
4. created when parts of an artwork spread out from a center point
5. a sense of motion in an artwork
6. how the parts of an artwork relate to each other
7. the measurement of objects against a common standard
8. the principle of design that creates a sense of wholeness and completeness
9. the importance given to certain objects or areas in an artwork
10. the technique of arranging an artwork so that no one part overpowers the others

Artists and Their Art

B Match the artist and artwork in the box with the subject and art concept below.

> Minnie Evans, *Design Made at Airlie Gardens*
> Jacob Lawrence, *Harriet Tubman Series No. 7*
> Mary Cassatt, *Motherhood*
> Hale Woodruff, *Georgia Landscape*
> Joseph Cornell, *Box with Objects*
> Philip Taaffe, *North African Strip*
> Victor Vasarely, *Vega-Nor*
> Diana Ong, *Miss Liberty III (Orange)*
> Franz Marc, *The Monkey (Frieze)*
> Gustave Caillebotte, *Paris Street, Rainy Day*

1. one or more animals/unity
2. American symbol/alternating rhythm
3. geometric shapes/progressive rhythm
4. portrait/emphasis
5. circular shapes and forms/assemblage
6. wet weather/asymmetrical balance
7. North African lanterns/pattern
8. strong leader/altered proportion
9. people adorned/symmetrical balance
10. autumn scene/random rhythm

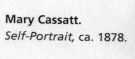

Mary Cassatt.
Self-Portrait, ca. 1878.

Hale Woodruff

Respond to Art

C Look at the painting *Still Life with a Curtain and Flowered Pitcher* by Paul Cézanne. In a class discussion or on a sheet of paper, match each art term below with examples from the painting.

Paul Cézanne. *Still Life with a Curtain and Flowered Pitcher*, 1899. Oil on canvas, 21 ½ by 29 ⅛ inches. Hermitage Museum, St. Petersburg, Russia.

Art Terms

1. balance
2. pattern
3. emphasis
4. unity
5. proportion
6. variety
7. rhythm
8. contrast

Unit 2 *Review*

Write About Art

Persuasive Paragraph

D Look back at the artworks in this unit. Choose the one you like best. Write a paragraph persuading readers that it is the best artwork in the unit. Copy the chart below and fill in the title of your favorite artwork. Beneath it, write two or three reasons why you think it is best and a detail from the artwork to support each reason. Use the completed chart to help you organize your paragraph.

(Title of Artwork)

Reason	Detail

Your Studio Work

E Answer these questions in your Sketchbook Journal or on a separate sheet of paper.

1. What skill or technique in this unit interested you or challenged you the most? Explain.
2. What problems did you have as you worked with new skills and techniques? How did you solve them? What will you do differently next time?
3. Which artworks inspired your own art-making process?
4. Choose one artwork to keep in your portfolio. Tell why you chose it.

Put It All Together

René Magritte. *Les Valeurs Personnelles (Personal Values),* 1952. Oil on canvas, 31 ½ by 39 ³⁄₈ inches. San Francisco Museum of Modern Art, San Francisco, CA.

F **Discuss or write about Magritte's painting *Les Valeurs Personnelles* using the four steps for critically viewing artwork.**

1. **Describe** What does this artwork show? Describe the objects.and their environment.

2. **Analyze** How did Magritte use the principles of design to create this artwork? Write several words about each principle listed below:
   Example: balance: asymmetrical; comb balances wardrobe

emphasis	**rhythm**	**unity**
proportion	**pattern**	**variety**

3. **Interpret** What do you think is the message of this artwork? What is the mood? What does it suggest about the artist's feelings about these objects?

4. **Judge** Belgian artist René Magritte (1898–1967) often made artworks that showed everyday objects in unexpected combinations and places. In this painting, did he succeed in making simple objects interesting? Explain.

"My painting is visible images which conceal nothing; they evoke mystery. . . ." —RENÉ MAGRITTE

Pablo Picasso. *Violin,* 1913–1914. Cardboard box, pasted papers, gouache, charcoal and chalk on cardboard, 20 ¹/₁₀ by 11 ⁹/₁₀ inches. Musée Picasso, Paris.

Unit 3

Art Media and Techniques

Artists use **art media,** or materials, to create artworks. In the same way musicians use their voices or play instruments, artists use methods, or **techniques,** to apply their media to create the artworks that you see.

Pablo Picasso used a variety of media and techniques to create his artworks. His techniques for applying these media included drawing, painting, and collage.

Many of the media and techniques you will learn about in this unit have been used for centuries. Most are still used by many of today's artists. You will discover how you can use and apply these media and techniques to create your own works of art.

Pablo Picasso. *Self-Portrait,* 1907.

About *the Artist*

Pablo Picasso is a well-known artist of the twentieth century. He had his first art exhibition when he was only sixteen. In his long career, Picasso explored a wide variety of art media and techniques. Discover more about the life and art of Picasso on pages 120–121.

Lesson 1

Drawing

Drawing is probably the first art process you tried as a child. Whether you simply doodle or create finished drawings, you may continue to draw all your life. People make drawings for many reasons. Have you ever made a quick drawing to show an idea that was hard to explain in words?

Artists often make drawings to help them plan other kinds of artworks, such as paintings or sculptures. A drawing made for this purpose is called a **study**. Inventions sometimes begin as drawings or studies. Certainly, there was a drawing of an airplane before there was an airplane.

Pencils, crayons, charcoal, markers, ink, and pastels are just some of the media that artists use for drawing. Using one **medium** or several media, an artist can express almost any subject, idea, or feeling through drawing.

Käthe Kollwitz. *Hand Studies.* Pen and ink and wash, 11 ½ by 9 inches. British Museum, London.

How did the artist use lines to create dark values?

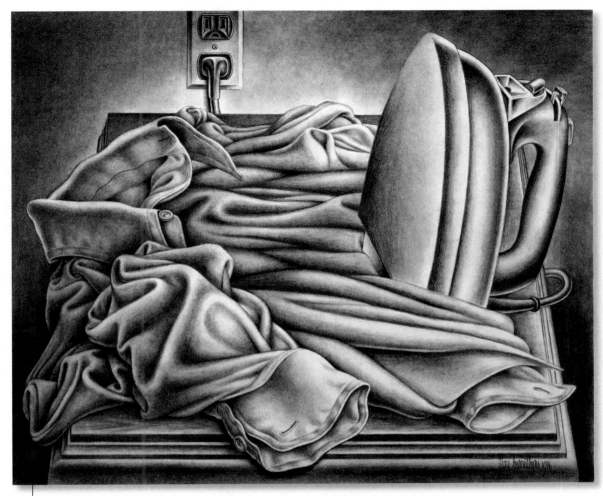

Roy Carruthers. *Ironing (Study),* 1976. Sepia drawing. © Roy Carruthers.

Drawing and Observing

Artists experiment with all kinds of media. South African artist Roy Carruthers (1938–) made the drawing above using sepia ink. Sepia was first made from ink produced by the cuttlefish.

Notice the subject of this drawing. Carruthers showed common objects familiar to most viewers. Notice his use of value and contrast. Why might an artist draw everyday scenes? Artists develop their skills by observing and drawing their surroundings. This practice improves artistic perception and awareness of the environment. You will find that observing your environment will also help you develop your drawing and artistic skills.

Sketchbook Journal

Make value charts using five different drawing media. Include pencil, crayon, charcoal, chalk pastel, and oil pastel. Divide a page into five sections. Use a different medium in each of the five sections to show value. Use the shading techniques of blending, hatching, cross-hatching, and stippling.

Vincent van Gogh. *Olive Trees at Montmajour,* 1888. Pencil, quill and reed pen with brown and black ink, 18 ¾ by 24 ⅕ inches. Musée des Beaux-Arts, Tournai, Belgium.

Why did the artist use more than one medium in this drawing?

This drawing by Dutch artist Vincent van Gogh (1853–1890) shows a **landscape,** or outdoor scene. To draw his **subject,** an olive grove, Van Gogh combined several drawing media. Read the credit line to see what media he used, and then notice these details:

- Van Gogh used black ink to draw the main objects and brown to add details.
- By using two colors, Van Gogh added depth, making the drawing more detailed and realistic.

Matching Medium and Subject

Review what you read about value and shading techniques in Unit 1, Lesson 6. Then look again at the drawing above. Describe the shading techniques Van Gogh used to create a range of values. Different drawing media allow the artist to make different types of lines. What makes ink a good medium for this subject?

Technique Tip

Using Markers

To avoid markers "bleeding," or spreading into unwanted areas, choose the right kind of drawing paper. Rough or porous papers, such as newsprint, are great for drawing with pencil, charcoal, and pastels. But these papers allow markers to spread. When using markers, choose a paper with a smoother surface.

Draw with Combined Media

Use what you have learned about drawing with combined media to draw a landscape.

Materials

✓ 12" × 18" white drawing paper
✓ 2 drawing media, such as a pencil and a marker

1 Choose two different drawing media to draw a landscape. Use your imagination or observation to create a landscape.

2 Use one medium or both media to draw the main lines and shapes in the landscape. Include various types of lines.

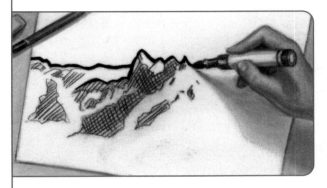

3 Apply shading techniques to show detail, texture, and a range of values.

Review and Reflect

- Describe your landscape and the objects you included.
- What types of lines and shading techniques did you use?
- How did the media you used affect the meaning of your landscape?
- Where did the media and techniques you used work best? Would you use different media next time? Explain.

Lesson 2

Painting

Thousands of years ago, animal fat was mixed with crushed, colored minerals to make the first paint. Today, paints are made by mixing pigments, or coloring agents, with a binder such as oil, wax, or glue. Binders make pigments stick together and to a surface. **Oil-based paint** has oil as a binder. **Water-based paints,** such as tempera, acrylics, and watercolors, have various binders that dissolve in water.

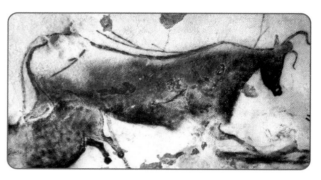

The cave paintings at Lascaux, France, are among the earliest known paintings.

Victor Vasarely. *Gestalt-Zoeld,* 1976. Acrylic on canvas, 93 ³/₅ by 87 ³/₄ inches. Private collection, Paris.

This painting uses pattern, color contrast, and value to show depth and directional change through shapes.

Janet Fish. *Stack of Plates,* 1980. Oil on canvas, 48 by 70 inches. Collection of the artist.
© Janet Fish/Licensed by VAGA, New York.

Painting Techniques

Read the credit line to see what kind of paint American artist Janet Fish (1938–) used in this artwork. Notice that the cups, plates, and other objects in the painting are well defined.

Oil paints dry more slowly than water-based paints. This way an artist can work more slowly to achieve the desired results. The thickness of oil paints also makes them easy to control. Although the paint is thick, Fish created the illusion of transparent glass.

To create many values of color in a painting, artists mix colors on a **palette.** A palette is a tray or board used by many artists to mix thick paints.

Sketchbook Journal

Make sketches of subjects you might paint with water-based paint and others you might paint with oil-based paint. Think about what you have learned about the qualities of the two kinds of paints. For each subject, write down which kind of paint you would use and why.

Diane Griffiths. *Lilith,* 1996. Watercolor and crayon. The Grand Design, Leeds, England.

What media did the artist combine to make this artwork?

Artists combine media in paintings to create a desired effect. In choosing media, artists think about the qualities of each medium and how they work together. Notice these details in *Lilith* by British artist Diane Griffiths (1957–):

- The artist combined crayon with watercolor. She knew that crayon wax and water do not mix, and she knew how this would affect her painting.
- Griffiths applied black and white crayons to darken and lighten certain areas of the painting.
- She used an opaque, or solid, medium first and then a transparent one. Think about why the order is important.
- Her choice of media allowed Griffiths to create bold, rhythmic lines and shapes as well as detailed patterns.

Resist Techniques

When artists combine media that do not mix, they are using a technique known as **resist.** One medium repels, or resists, the other to create a desired effect. Combining wax or wax-based media with water-based paint is a common resist technique.

Technique Tip

Experiment with Resist

Vary the pressure as you apply crayon to change the amount of paint resisted. Apply light pressure with the crayon to allow some of the paper to show through. To get an opaque effect, apply crayon solidly, using more pressure.

Studio 2

Paint with Combined Media

Use what you have learned about painting with combined media to paint a moonlit scene.

Materials

- ✓ 12" × 18" watercolor paper
- ✓ pencil
- ✓ crayons
- ✓ watercolors
- ✓ paintbrushes

1 Use a pencil to draw a moonlit scene on your paper. Choose areas to cover with black or dark blue crayon.

2 Keeping in mind how the moonlight will affect each object's appearance, use white crayon to highlight the areas that moonlight might strike. Use watercolors to fill the scene.

3 After the paint has dried, use crayons to add details to your painting.

Review and Reflect

- Describe the scene you painted.
- Why did you choose the areas you did for the resist technique? What effect did your choices have on the painting?
- What does your resist painting express about moonlit nights?
- What impact do you think your painting will have on its viewers? Why?

Lesson 3

Printmaking

Printmaking allows artists to achieve unique effects or make multiple copies from a single design. The idea is to transfer an image from a printing **plate** or **block** covered with wet color to another surface. The artist often applies the color, usually ink, with a **brayer,** a simple tool that rolls ink on evenly. Then a surface such as paper is applied to the plate or block. The paper picks up ink from the plate to make a print of the image. The artist then pulls the print.

A brayer allows for an even application of ink to a printing plate or block.

Barry Wilson. *Moon Rooster.* Woodcut print, 26 by 22 ½ inches. Private collection.

Notice the patterns and textures the artist created by carving them into the wood block.

Rembrandt van Rijn. *Landscape with Three Trees,* 1643. Etching, 8 by 10 inches. Musée Condé, Chantilly, France.

Plates and Prints

Artists make plates for printing out of many different materials. The plate for the woodcut print on page 112 was a piece of wood. What kind of plate do you think is used for a linoleum cut print? When a polished stone is used as a plate, the resulting print is a **lithograph.**

This print by Dutch artist Rembrandt van Rijn (1606–1669) is an **etching.** The plate was a sheet of copper covered with a layer of wax. Rembrandt drew the image into the wax and then bathed the plate in acid. The acid ate into the plate where the lines were drawn, and then the wax was removed. Next, the artist inked the plate and made a print on paper. Which areas of the print were not etched by the acid?

Research

Do online research to learn more about different printmaking processes. Use the words *printmaking history* as keywords for your search. Learn how printmaking has changed through time. What are the oldest methods? How has technology affected printmaking processes?

M. C. Escher. *Rippled Surface,* 1950. Linoleum cut in black and grey-brown, printed from 2 blocks, 10 ¼ by 12 ⅝ inches. © 2003 Cordon Art B.V., Baarn, Holland. All rights reserved.

How did the artist represent ripples on water?

Dutch printmaker M. C. Escher (1898–1972) used two printing blocks to create this print. Try to imagine each block as you read below.

- One block printed the black areas and the second printed the grey-brown areas. Which of the two blocks created the negative space?
- The images on the blocks were mirror images of what appears in the print. Think about why that is true.
- The reflection of the moon is an area of the block that did not receive ink. Is the moon's reflection positive or negative space?

Intaglio and Relief Prints

An **intaglio print** is made by cutting or scratching an image into a surface. The cut grooves are filled with ink. Then the plate is pressed onto the paper hard enough

that the paper goes into the grooves and picks up the ink. In **relief prints,** such as this one by Escher, the area to be inked is raised above the surface of the printing block. The other parts of the surface are removed with various tools. The inked block is then pressed onto the paper.

Technique Tip

Mirror Images

To help you create plates for making prints, experiment with mirror images. Draw some simple designs that you think would make interesting prints. View each design in a mirror. Pay close attention to how the mirror image differs from the original.

Studio 3

Make a Relief Print

Use what you have learned to create a relief print of a real or imagined outdoor scene or animal, using two printing plates.

Materials

- ✓ 9" × 12" drawing paper and pencil
- ✓ two 9" × 12" pieces of sturdy cardboard
- ✓ cardboard pieces
- ✓ scissors and utility knife ⚠
- ✓ glue
- ✓ 9" × 12" white or colored paper
- ✓ heavy string or yarn
- ✓ printing ink or tempera paint
- ✓ brayer and inking surface

1 Draw a design for your print using simple shapes. Use your design to draw and cut out shapes for the first printing plate from cardboard.

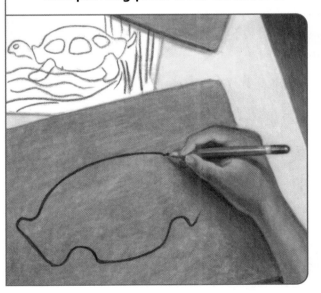

2 Glue the cutout cardboard shapes to a 9" × 12" piece of cardboard. Use a brayer to ink the plate. Press the paper over the plate and pull your print.

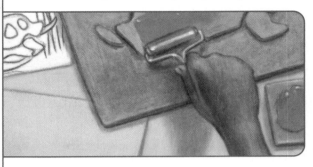

3 Create a second printing plate to add details, using string and glue. Ink the second plate. Gently press your print over the second plate. Pull your print.

Review and Reflect

- Describe the lines and shapes in your print.
- How did using two printing plates affect your design? How do the colors, lines, and shapes work together?
- What mood or feeling does your print convey about your subject?
- Would the addition of more details improve your print? Explain.

Collage

When Pablo Picasso glued a piece of oilcloth to one of his paintings, a new technique was born. The word **collage** comes from the French word *coller,* meaning "to glue or to paste." In the technique of collage, the artist glues chosen materials onto a flat surface. Materials may include pieces of cut or torn paper, photographs, fabric, text and images cut from publications, or other found objects that can be glued. This collage by Kurt Schwitters shows the variety of materials that can be used.

Kurt Schwitters. *Merz Picture 32A. Cherry Picture,* 1921. Collage of cloth, wood, metal, gouache, oil, cut-and-pasted papers, and ink on cardboard, 36 1/8 by 27 3/4 inches. The Museum of Modern Art, New York.

John Piper. *Littlestone-on-Sea,* 1936. Collage, paper and ink. Tate Gallery, London.

Collage and Expression

British artist John Piper (1903–1992) created this collage using cut and torn papers. His use of torn paper adds to the composition by building up the surface and creating different textures. How did Piper use ink in this collage? The title tells you that the subject of the collage is a town by the sea. What message do you think Piper wanted to express about the place?

The technique of collage allows artists to use a variety of shapes, lines, and textures to create a unified composition. Other artists use collage to express ideas or moods about a subject or convey a personal message.

Sketchbook Journal

What message would you like to express using the technique of collage? Draw some ideas for messages that you want to convey. Make notes about the media and colors you would use to convey your message. Collect a few samples and paste them into your Sketchbook Journal with your notes.

Mixed-Media *Collage*

Freshman Brown. *Guitar Player*, 1999. Mixed media and collage. © Freshman Brown.

Why do you think the artist used paint in this collage?

What helps you recognize the subject of this collage by American artist Freshman Brown (1940–)? The artist used more than one medium, or **mixed media,** to convey his message about a guitar player. Look for these details:

- The overlapping combination of torn papers adds visual texture.
- The use of different media adds visual interest.
- The painted blue of the guitar player's shirt creates emphasis and a focal point.

Choosing and Using Media

Some artists plan their media carefully before beginning their collages. Others let their imaginations run wild. Consider what message or feeling you want to convey. Then choose a variety of media that will make your collage and message pop!

Technique Tip

Collage Materials

Make a distinction between "ripping" and "tearing" when you are not cutting paper for a collage. For small pieces, use both hands to make a small tear, and move them to a new position before you continue. Work slowly to get the shape you want. For larger pieces, place one hand flat as a guide and pull the paper with a long, smooth motion.

Studio 4

Make a Mixed-Media Collage

Use what you have learned about collage to create an artwork showing yourself in a favorite place.

Materials

- ✓ paper and fabric scraps
- ✓ scissors ⑤
- ✓ glue
- ✓ tempera paints
- ✓ paintbrushes
- ✓ markers

1 Picture yourself in your favorite place. How can you show this in a collage?

2 Choose papers and fabrics to show you and your favorite place.

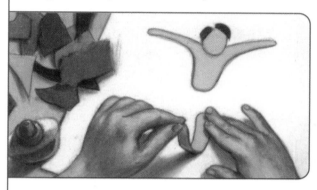

3 Use tempera paint to add details. After it dries, add more details using markers.

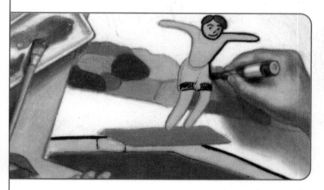

Review and Reflect

- Describe your favorite place. What types of lines and shapes did you use to show it?
- Why did you use each medium as you did? Which principle of design stands out most in your collage?
- What mood does your collage suggest? What title will you give it? Why?
- Where would you like to hang your collage? Why?

119

Meet *the Artist*

Pablo Picasso

Picasso's father was a painter and an art teacher. He recognized his son's talent early, and Picasso's art training began while he was very young. By age eleven he was taking classes at art school. He was already exhibiting his artwork while still a teenager.

As an adult, Picasso continued to go beyond the expected. He was an artist of great talent, daring, and inventiveness. His long and varied career made him one of the well-known and influential artists of the twentieth century.

Pablo Picasso. *Self-Portrait,* 1907. Oil on canvas, approximately 21 4/5 by 17 ½ inches. National Gallery, Prague, Czech Republic.

"I am always doing that which I cannot do, in order that I may learn how to do it." —PABLO PICASSO

This self-portrait is an early example of Picasso's Cubist painting.

The Coming of Cubism

Pablo Picasso was born in Spain but spent most of his life in France. As a young artist, he was influenced by the works of French painters Toulouse-Lautrec and Georges Seurat. Between 1901 and 1904, Picasso explored shades of blue in his paintings, and those years became known as his Blue Period.

When he was twenty-five, Picasso painted his first Cubist artwork. In this new art style, Picasso showed people and objects from different angles all at once. He changed perspective and distorted figures. Cubism was so different from other artwork of the time that it shocked both other artists and the public.

Media and Experimentation

Over the years, Picasso continued to develop his Cubist style. He also worked with fellow artist Georges Braque to develop a new art technique, which they called collage. While he produced many drawings and paintings, Picasso was always eager to express his creativity in new ways. He created many sculptures, working in wood, plaster, clay, and even cardboard. He designed the set and costumes for a ballet. Many years later he wrote a play and also published poetry. Picasso lived until he was ninety-one, and he explored new ways of artistic expression throughout his life.

Talk About It

- Why do you think Picasso lived most of his life in France, rather than remaining in Spain?

- About how old was Picasso when he painted *Guernica?*

The Life of Picasso

Pablo Picasso

Georges Braque

1880

1881
Pablo Picasso
born in Malaga, Spain
(October 25)

Picasso moves to
Barcelona, attends
School of Fine Arts
1896

1900
Picasso begins to spend time
in France; paints in the
Post Impressionist style

1901
Picasso's Blue
Period begins

1905

1907
Picasso founds
Cubist movement

1912
Picasso and Georges
Braque create collage

1930

1937
Picasso finishes
painting *Guernica*

1941
Picasso writes a play

1955

1973
Picasso dies, Mougius,
France (April 8)

1980

Look *and Compare*

Collages from Two Eras

Artists constantly develop new ways to use art media. Different media, styles, and subjects of paintings have been popular at different times and places. Collages show the media, styles, and subjects of the times in which they were created.

The technique of collage often includes the use of a variety of media and objects.

A Collage by the Inventor

The Picasso collage on page 123 combines the collage technique with the Cubist style. Notice how the figures and objects are broken apart and abstracted. Picasso painted many of the papers he used in this collage, adding pattern and texture. The repeated patterns and neutral colors unify the composition. Picasso made the center figure the focal point by making her a different color. What principles of design are achieved by Picasso's use of red?

A More Modern Collage

Picasso's collage technique is used today by artists all over the world. American artist Robert Rauschenberg (1925–) used some of the same media and techniques as Picasso, yet the collage is very different. Like many collages today, Rauschenberg's composition includes found objects, such as fabric, metal, and rubber. Describe the different objects that you can identify in Rauschenberg's collage. Then look for the different materials in the artwork. How do the different materials add variety and interest?

Although each artist's media are different, the results are similar. Notice how Picasso's use of paint and torn papers creates visual texture. Rauschenberg used wood, fabric, and paint to create texture. How would these artworks be different if the artists had used only paint?

Pablo Picasso. *Women at Their Toilettes,* 1938.
Paper, gouache, and painted paper collage.
Musée Picasso, Paris.

Robert Rauschenberg. *Reservoir,* 1961.
Oil, wood, graphite, fabric, metal, and rubber
on canvas, 85 ½ by 62 ½ by 14 ¾ inches.
Smithsonian American Art Museum,
Washington, D.C.

Compare & Contrast

- Describe the subjects of the two collages. What elements unify each collage?

- Compare these collages to the one on page 118. What do all three have in common?

Textile Arts

A T-shirt is just a T-shirt until you paint it or tie-dye it or sew beads onto it. Then it's a work of art! **Textiles** are artworks made from cloth or from fibers, such as yarn, thread, and cord. Textile artists use these media and others to create their works of art. **Batik** is a form of textile art that uses the resist technique that you read about in Lesson 2. A design is created on fabric with the application of melted wax, and then the fabric is dyed.

Artist unknown, Chinese. *Bridal Robe with Butterfly Design,* 19th century. Wool, silk embroidery, satin sleeve bands, 50 ½ by 48 ½ inches. Collection of The Newark Museum, Newark, NJ.

Notice the patterns and details the artist applied to this robe using textile arts.

Agueda Martínez. *Tapestry Weave Rag Jerga,* 1994. Woven cotton cloth on cotton yarn warp, 86 ½ by 52 ½ inches. Smithsonian American Art Museum, Washington, D.C.

Woven Art

Look closely at the clothes you are wearing. They probably include machine-woven fibers or threads. Many fiber artists weave fabrics and fibers by hand. The art of **weaving** involves interlocking fibers to create a piece of fabric.

Navajo-Mexican artist Agueda Martínez was born in 1898. She used cotton fibers to weave this tapestry when she was in her mid-nineties. Unlike today's fabrics, it was made by hand on a **loom,** which holds the fibers in position as they are woven. **Warp** fibers run lengthwise. **Weft** fibers are woven over and under the warp fibers. Is the fringe at either end of the weaving created by the warp or the weft fibers?

Visual Culture

Take a look around you at all the fabrics in your environment. Examine fabrics used to make clothing, towels, upholstery, and other objects. Consider how each fabric was made. Try to determine which are hand-woven and which are machine-made. Look for the warp and weft fibers. Find details that add interest.

Studio 5 Setup
Quilt *Designs*

Michael James. *Rehoboth Meander: Quilt #150,* 1993. Cotton and silk, 52 ½ by 52 inches. Renwick Gallery, Smithsonian American Art Museum, Washington, D.C.

How is this quilt like and unlike other quilts you have seen?

Quilts are a form of **stitchery,** created using a needle, thread or yarn, and fabric. To make a quilt, an artist sews together two layers of cloth with padding in between. Quilt artists may create complex designs or simple patterns. The quilt on this page was made by American artist Michael James (1949–). Look for these details:

- The artist's design includes a geometric pattern created by diagonal lines.
- The repeated organic shapes create positive and negative space.
- The combination of organic and geometric shapes adds a sense of rhythm.

Quilting Techniques

Appliqué is the technique of stitching or sewing fabric onto a fabric background. The term comes from a French word meaning "to put on." Using the appliqué technique in quilt-making is another way to add detail. Quilts also have thousands of tiny stitches made both for decoration and to hold the layers of the quilt together.

Technique Tip
Keyboard Shortcuts

If you use a computer to design patterns for quilts or other artworks, take advantage of the tools the program has to offer. Most software drawing programs include tools that can save time when you create patterns. These tools allow you to create lines and shapes, fill shapes or the background with color, and repeat these lines and shapes to create patterns. Some programs even provide tools for adding patterns.

Studio 5

Design a Quilt

Use what you have learned about textile art to create a quilt design.

Materials

- ✓ computer with drawing software
- ✓ color printer
- ✓ printer paper

1 Use computer drawing software to draw a rectangle large enough to fill the printer paper you are using.

2 Create a design for your quilt. You may want to make a block design or a free-form design.

3 Experiment with different color schemes. When you are satisfied with the color scheme, save and print out your design.

Review and Reflect

- Describe your quilt design. What elements of art did you include?
- What techniques of fiber art would you use to make this quilt from fabric?
- What kind of message or story does your quilt design tell?
- Would you use your quilt for a functional or decorative purpose? Why?

Lesson 6

Sculpture

Would you ever consider a piñata as a type of sculpture? **Sculptures** are three-dimensional forms made by modeling, carving, or assembling materials. Artists create sculptures using a variety of media and techniques. They may use clay, wood, metal, stone, or a combination of these. Like a piñata, some sculptures are made from **papier-mâché,** which is the process of covering a framework with strips of paper soaked in a thin paste. The paste then dries, creating a hard surface suitable for painting or decorating with materials such as found objects.

There are two basic kinds of sculpture. Sculpture in the round is a freestanding form meant to be viewed from all sides. Relief sculpture shows forms that project from a background. The sculpture of Theodore Roosevelt is an example of **bas-relief,** or low relief, because the form projects only slightly from the background. It was made by a process called **casting.** American sculptor Sally James Farnham (1876–1943) first made a wax model of her subject. Next, she covered the model with a heat-proof mold. She then melted the wax, poured it out, and poured melted bronze into the mold.

Sally James Farnham. *Theodore Roosevelt (1858–1919). 26th President of the U.S.,* 1906. Bronze relief, 20 11/16 by 20 11/16 inches. National Portrait Gallery, Smithsonian Institution, Washington, D.C.

Artist unknown, Toltec. *Warrior Columns on Pyramid B,* ca. A.D. 1008. Tula, Mexico.

The warriors, or *atlantes,* that these columns represent are shown dressed for battle.

Sculpting Techniques

The Toltec people of Mexico flourished between about A.D. 900 and 1250. Their capital, Tula, was about forty miles from present-day Mexico City. These columns stand atop the ruins of the main pyramid at Tula. What purpose might these columns have served? The Toltecs probably created the columns using the **subtractive method.** In this technique, pieces of stone are carved away to create the final design. Some artists also use the subtractive method to sculpt clay.

Another technique, known as the **additive method,** involves adding materials, such as clay, to create a sculpture. Notice the patterns and details the Toltecs achieved in their sculptures. How might patterns be created using the additive method?

Sketchbook Journal

Sculptures are common in public places, such as parks, libraries, and government buildings. Notice the sculptures you see in your community. Choose one that you like and make a sketch of it. Include notes about the media and techniques you think the artist used.

Leo Sewell. *Stegosaurus,* 1984. Found objects, 14 by 7 by 20 feet. Created for the West Palm Beach Science Museum. © Leo Sewell.

What objects can you identify in this artwork?

Some sculptors, like American artist Leo Sewell, use found objects in their sculptures. You read in Unit 2 that artists often combine found objects to create an assemblage. Similar to some clay sculptures, assemblages are created using the additive method, in which found objects are added or attached to one another. Look for these details in Sewell's assembled sculpture:

- The colors and shapes of the recycled objects add variety to the sculpture.
- The use of found objects gives the sculpture a variety of textures.
- The objects are assembled in such a way as to make them appear like a solid surface.
- The repeated shapes on the animal's back create a pattern.

Assembly Methods

Artists use various methods to assemble materials for sculptures. In some sculptures, objects are glued, wired, nailed, or bolted together. In other artworks, artists begin with an **armature,** or frame, to which they attach the materials and objects.

Technique Tip

Subassemblies
Avoid watching your assemblage fall apart before your eyes! Plan your work in stages and allow glued pieces to dry separately. Work on one area or piece of the whole and set it aside to dry. Later, put the various subassemblies together to make your finished project.

Studio 6

Make a Sculpture with Found Objects

Use what you have learned about sculpture to make one from found objects.

Materials

- ✓ 12" × 18" newsprint
- ✓ pencil
- ✓ collection of small found objects
- ✓ pipe cleaners, yarn, ribbon, beads, aluminum foil
- ✓ masking or other tape (optional)
- ✓ glue and wire
- ✓ wood for base

1 Plan a design for your sculpture. You may choose to sculpt an animal or other object.

2 Use glue to assemble your found objects. Use tape to hold heavier objects in place as the glue dries.

3 Use beads, yarn, foil, and other materials to add details. Attach your sculpture to a base and sign it.

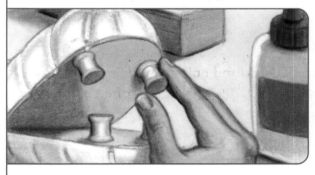

Review and Reflect

- Describe the shapes and forms you used to create your sculpture. What type of sculpture is it?
- Why did you choose the found objects you used? How do the shapes and forms add interest to your sculpture?
- How does your sculpture reveal your feelings about the subject?
- What is the best feature of your sculpture? Why?

Lesson 7

Architecture

You have read that inventions often begin as drawings. The same is true of buildings. **Architecture** is the art and science of planning and drawing buildings and other environmental features. Some **architects** design buildings and living spaces. **Landscape architects** design outdoor spaces such as private and public gardens, golf courses, and theme parks.

Ictinus and Callicrates, architects. *Parthenon,* ca. 447–432 B.C. Athens, Greece.

Postnik Yakovlev, architect.
St. Basil's Cathedral (Petrovsky Cathedral), 1555–1561.
Moscow, Russia.

Architecture and Expression

A building's design reflects many elements: the time and place at which it is designed, the purpose for which it will be built, and the architect's personal style. Russian architect Postnik Yakovlev designed St. Basil's Cathedral for Ivan IV, the first czar of Russia. This church is famous for its graceful towers and colorful design. It was built to celebrate victory over the city of Kazan, about four hundred miles east of Moscow. Each of the cathedral's towers commemorates a battle against Kazan. How does the cathedral compare to buildings in your community?

Visual Culture

Notice the architectural style of buildings in your community, such as your favorite restaurant or store. As you look at each building, consider when it was built. Make notes about what you see and how newer buildings compare to older ones.

Studio 7 Setup
A Home *for Art*

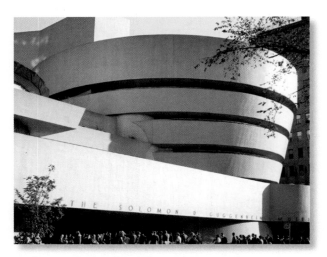

Frank Lloyd Wright, architect. *Solomon R. Guggenheim Museum (Exterior),* 1956–1959. New York.

Frank Lloyd Wright, architect. *Solomon R. Guggenheim Museum (Interior),* 1956–1959. New York.

What design elements do the exterior and interior of the museum share?

Frank Lloyd Wright (1867–1959), an influential American architect of the twentieth century, felt that buildings should fit well in their environments. He developed a style known as *organic architecture.*

- Notice the organic shapes in this building, such as its flowing curved wall.
- Inside, plenty of natural light makes this a good home for artworks.
- The circular design provides plenty of display space.

Stages of a Building

A building is a complex artwork that goes through several stages of construction. These stages are first combined in a set of plans called blueprints. **Blueprints** are detailed drawings that show a builder how to construct the building. These include a floor plan and various elevations, or outside views. In addition, an architect often makes a model of the building.

Technique Tip

Drawing in Proportion

Use graph paper to draw architectural plans. This will help you draw in proportion to the actual building. Determine the distance each square of the graph paper will represent. For instance, one square may equal ten feet of the building. Then calculate how many squares you need for each length.

Studio 7

Create a Museum Plan

Use what you have learned about architecture to design an art museum.

Materials

- ✓ sketchpad
- ✓ pencil
- ✓ graph paper, several sheets
- ✓ ruler

1 Draw several floor plans and elevation designs for an art museum. Include galleries, offices, a restaurant, a gift shop, and restrooms.

2 Finalize your designs and use a ruler to draw them to scale on graph paper. Label everything clearly.

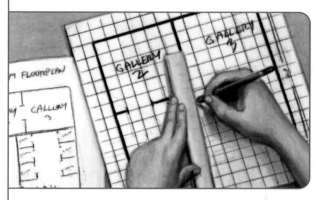

3 Draw a landscape design for the museum grounds. Keep it to scale as well.

Review and Reflect

- Describe the elements you used in your museum design.
- What building materials would you use to construct your museum?
- What kinds of artwork would be at home in this museum?
- What would you change if you revised the design?

Lesson 8

Ceramics and Pottery

Ceramics, or pottery, is one of the world's oldest art forms. For as long as people have made objects to drink from, carry, and cook with, they have made them decorative as well as functional. They shaped clay into graceful forms, hardened it with heat, and decorated it with paints and glazes.

Archaeologists study pottery made by artists all over the world to learn about their lives and their cultures. They study the shapes and forms of the pottery to understand the purpose for which it was made. The designs help provide information about the media and symbols the artists used. Notice the forms and patterns in the pottery below. Today, potters, artists who create pottery, use some of the same media and techniques.

Artist unknown, Aztec. *Eating bowl and cups.* British Museum, London.

Artist unknown. *Tomb figure of a horse,* Tang Dynasty (A.D. 618–907). Pottery. Idemitsu Museum of Art, Tokyo, Japan.

Decorative Pottery

The Aztec pottery on the previous page is an example of **applied art,** meaning it was created to be useful or functional. The ceramic horse, made during China's Tang Dynasty, is an example of decorative art. Most **decorative art** is made to be viewed.

The Chinese artist shaped the body of the horse above and then added parts of the saddle and decorations one piece at a time. When the artist was finished making the sculpture, he or she applied glazes. Look for places where the glaze dripped or ran when the sculpture was heated. Where did the artist apply patterns?

Sketchbook Journal

Make several sketches of both applied and decorative art that you would like to create. As you draw each piece, consider what function or purpose it will serve. Include notes with each sketch that describe how the object might be used and the process you would use to create it.

Maria Montoya Martinez. *Bowl.* Blackware, 6 ¾ by 9 ½ inches. Smithsonian American Art Museum, Washington, D.C.

During the firing process, the fire's oxygen supply was cut off, causing the smoke to blacken the bowl.

Artists who make pottery often use materials and techniques that are unique to their location or culture. Native American artist Maria Montoya Martinez (ca. 1880–1980) gathered and mixed clay and volcanic ash found near her home to make this bowl. She rolled the clay into ropes, or coils, to form the bowl, and then fired or baked it at a high temperature in a handmade oven. Notice these details:

- Though built from coiled ropes of clay, the finished bowl is smooth. The abstract design includes geometric and organic shapes.
- Martinez polished the fired clay with a stone to create a shiny finish. The contrast of the dull and shiny textures makes the design more interesting.

Function and Beauty

As potters have done through the ages, Martinez made her bowl both functional and decorative. Think of ways that the bowl might have been used. If you made a ceramic bowl, how would you use it, and how would you shape and decorate it to reflect your life?

Technique Tip

Coil Technique
To create clay coils, roll pieces of clay between your hands and a covered tabletop to make ropes that are about one-half inch thick and several inches long. Then, to connect ropes into a coil, first score the surfaces and add slip to cement them together.

Make Functional Pottery

Use what you have learned about pottery to make a functional piece for yourself or a friend.

Materials

✓ ceramic clay and slip
✓ clay tools
✓ found objects (optional)
✓ kiln (optional) ⚠
✓ glaze or acrylic paints

1 Use the coil technique to make a piece of pottery, such as a jar or a bowl. Use a slab of clay for the bottom of your pottery.

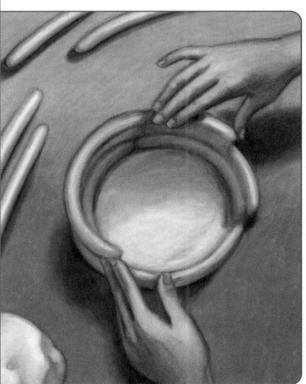

2 Use clay tools or found objects to scratch or press designs into your pottery.

3 Let your pottery dry completely. Fire it and then paint it with acrylic paint or glaze. Fire it again if glaze is used.

Review and Reflect

- What words best describe the shape of your pottery?
- How did you use lines, shapes, and textures to create a design?
- How does the shape of your pottery reveal its function? Do the designs you added help reveal the function? Explain.
- Which part of the process do you think was most successful? Explain.

Lesson 9

Photography and Videography

Some of the media that you have read about have been around for thousands of years. **Still photography** is a much newer medium. The first photograph was taken in 1826, less than two hundred years ago. **Videography,** art made with a video camera, is even newer.

Photographers and videographers continue to develop new techniques for using these media. Like other artists, they consider the elements of art and principles of design when composing their images. Timing is also an important factor. Look at the two photographs on this page. American photographer Margaret Bourke-White (1904–1971) captured the image of an airplane flying into a dark sky. NASA mission specialist Gregory Harbaugh (1956–) was floating in space when he composed the bottom photograph. Notice what type of balance each photograph shows.

Margaret Bourke-White. *B-36 at High Altitude, Flying Over Wichita, Kansas,* 1951. Silver gelatin print.

Gregory Harbaugh, NASA mission specialist. *Dark Sky, Bright Sun,* February, 1997. Digital photograph.

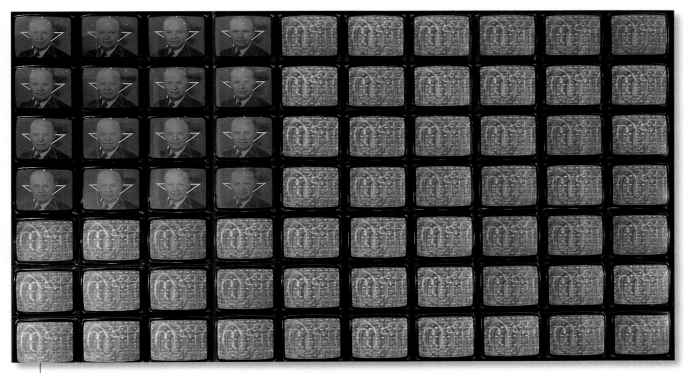

Nam June Paik. *Video Flag*, 1985–1996. 70 video monitors, 4 laser disc players, computer, timers, electrical devices, wood and metal housing on rubber wheels, 94 ³/₈ by 139 ³/₄ by 47 ³/₄ inches. Hirshhorn Museum and Sculpture Garden, Smithsonian Institution, Washington, D.C.

Videography and Expression

When the camera was first invented, some people thought that photography could never be art. All a camera could do was record what was in front of the lens, they said. Photographers soon proved them wrong. They used the camera, the developing process, and photographs in unexpected ways. Later, videography broadened the opportunities for expression.

American artist Nam June Paik (1932–) combines videography, computers, and other technologies to create artworks such as *Video Flag*. The videos constantly change, showing the stars and stripes, news stills, the Statue of Liberty, and faces of past presidents. What message do you think Paik wanted to express with this artwork?

Research

Use online or library sources to learn about the history and technology of photography. Discover who made the first camera and how it worked. Learn about the history and processes for developing and manipulating film. How has photography changed over time? What brought about the changes?

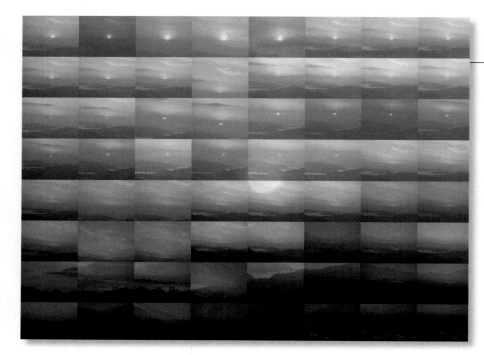

Ryan Li. *Sunrise Montage,* 2001. Photomontage, 21 ⅓ by 16 inches. © Ryan Li.

The artist created this photomontage using digital images and a computer software program.

How many images did photographer Ryan Li include in this **photomontage,** or collage of combined photographs? The photographs each show a portion of a specific landscape at sunrise. The artist's use of digital media allowed him to manipulate and combine the photographs into a unified composition. Notice these details:

- Each photograph reflects the theme of the photomontage.
- The repeated colors in the combined photographs help unify the composition.

Expressive Photography

For Ryan Li, capturing images on film or digitally is all about getting the right shot at the right time. "Missing it means there may never be another chance to retake a shot," says Li. "For me, every photo I take is part of my visual experience of life." Do you think this photomontage reflects Li's thoughts and feelings about taking photographs? Why or why not?

Technique Tip

Camera Options

A digital camera allows you to see what photographs will look like before they are printed. Digital images can be changed using a computer. A camera with self-developing film also works well. These cameras give you "instant" photographs. Either camera is a good option for photomontages.

Studio 9

Make a Photomontage

Use what you have learned about photography to make a photomontage.

Materials

- ✓ digital camera (optional)
- ✓ computer and printer (optional)
- ✓ magazine photographs
- ✓ personal photographs (optional)
- ✓ posterboard or heavy paper
- ✓ glue

1 Take several photographs of your chosen subject and upload them to a computer, or cut out photographs from magazines.

2 Use the computer to arrange your images into a pleasing composition, or arrange the magazine photographs in the same manner.

3 Print your photomontage using a printer, or use glue to attach the magazine photographs to the posterboard.

Review and Reflect

- Discuss the colors, lines, shapes, and textures in your photomontage. Describe the subject.
- How did you choose what photos to use and how to arrange them?
- How do the photographs in your artwork relate to the theme and subject of your photomontage?
- What makes your photomontage successful?

Lesson 10

Computer Art

The people who built the first computer most likely did not know that they were also inventing a new art tool. Computers were first used for mathematical calculations and processing data. Artists soon saw the possibilities of using these ever-changing machines as a medium for creating artworks, or **computer arts.**

Karin Kuhlmann (1948–) is a German artist who discovered the computer as an art medium in 1994. "I gained the necessary knowledge for it in a self-taught manner," she says. Kuhlmann uses a variety of computer **software,** or applications, to draw, paint, arrange, and alter images. *Approach* was created with software that allows her to give objects the appearance of having three dimensions, or form. "For me, as a photographer," she says, "it is very interesting to arrange a scene according to my own ideas."

Karin Kuhlmann. *Approach,* 1997. 3D-Computer Art, 14 4/5 by 19 9/10 inches. Collection of the artist.

Harold Cohen. *Untitled (Bathers Series),* 1986.
Computer-drawn image, hand-painted with
acrylic on canvas, 100 by 67 inches. Collection
of Bob Hendel.

Creative Computers

Imagine having a computer create an
artwork for you! British artist Harold Cohen
(1928–) did just that with his invention
of AARON, a computer program that the
artist designed to draw lines and shapes.
Cohen's drawing program can also create
fairly realistic drawings of flowers and other
plants, as well as repeated shapes. Where
do you notice repeated shapes in this
drawing by AARON? The diagonal lines
of the trees help give the illusion that the
figures are moving forward. The many
colors include tints and shades and add
interest and variety. What is the focal point
of the artwork?

Sketchbook Journal

**Use a computer drawing
program to make a simple sketch
of yourself. Use the program's
tools to help you repeat shapes
and move things around. As you
draw, take notes about the tools
you used to achieve different
results. Write down ideas about
how you might use the
computer for an artwork.**

Shrek and the Donkey (still image from animated movie, Shrek), 2001. Computer animated characters.

It took three hundred artists to create all the animations for the movie *Shrek*.

Computer animation is the process of using a computer to create moving images and characters. Notice these details about Shrek and the donkey:

- In the science of computer animation, realistic details such as hair and fur are important. Evaluate how realistic *Shrek* animators made such details.
- Making characters look interesting and likable, or not so likable if they are villains, is also important. Note these characters' expressions.

Computer Animation Techniques

Some computer animators do all their work on the computer, from original sketches to finished animation. Others draw on paper and use a scanner to upload drawings to the computer. Once in the computer, the drawings are stored as digital images. In electronic files, digital images are large numbers of digits representing locations and colors of dots, or pixels, that form an image.

Technique Tip

Save Everything

One of the great powers of the computer is that it lets you copy, revise, rename, and reuse parts of your work. Before you delete something that you have decided does not work, save it in a separate file on the desktop. Keep the file open as you work. You may come back to it after trying something else, or you may end up using it in another project.

Create a Computer Animation

Use what you have learned about computer animation to try it yourself.

Materials

- ✓ drawing paper
- ✓ markers
- ✓ computer with scanner and drawing software

1 Make four drawings of a character at different stages of action, such as swinging a bat. Be sure to include a background. Add color with markers.

2 Scan the drawings into a computer and use drawing software to add 3-D effects.

3 Use the program's copy feature to help you create additional images of the character at various stages of action.

Review and Reflect

- Describe the character and the action in your animation.
- How did you use lines and color to show the character's movement?
- What story or scene does your animation tell or depict?
- What would be a good title for your animation? Why?

Create a Mixed-Media Triptych

Amy Cain. *I Don't Remember My Dreams #2, #3, & #4 (triptych),* 1998. Oil, wax, mother-of-pearl, copper foil, and ink on wood, 13 by 12 inches. © 1998 Amy Cain.

Plan

A **triptych** is an artwork that has three panels. The panels may be joined together, or they may be separate pieces that are displayed side by side. The three parts of a triptych go together in some way representing a unified idea, theme, or image. Artist Amy Cain used mixed media and a variety of techniques to create each panel of this triptych. Look for these details:

- What makes the three parts go together, giving the triptych unity?
- What is the subject of the artwork? What do you think Cain wanted to express about the subject?
- What would you like to express in a triptych? How could you use some of the media and techniques you have read about to express your ideas and feelings?

Using your knowledge of media and techniques, create your own mixed-media triptych.

Sketchbook Journal

Choose a subject that you would like to show in a triptych. Think about three different images or examples of the subject that you would show. Make some sketches showing different ideas for your triptych. Make notes about the media you might use for each panel.

Materials

✓ three pieces of 12" × 18" white posterboard or foam core
✓ drawing media
✓ painting media
✓ collage materials and glue
✓ masking tape

1 Plan each panel of your triptych. Use mixed media on at least two panels. Include drawing, painting, and collage techniques in your artwork.

2 On each piece of posterboard, draw the design that will appear on that panel. Decide the order of your panels. Show unity between the three panels.

3 Use the media and techniques from this unit to complete each panel of the triptych.

4 Attach the panels together by applying masking tape to the two side panels and the center panel. Be sure to sign your finished artwork.

Reflect

- What problems did you have while completing your triptych? How did you solve them?
- In what ways did the media and techniques you used help you express your ideas?
- What did you discover about the media and techniques you used?
- Talk to a classmate about the project. How are your triptychs the same? How are they different?

149

Unit 3 *Review*

Vocabulary Review

A Match each art term below with its definition.

> textile ✔
> architecture ✔
> collage ✔
> photomontage
> medium ✔
>
> intaglio ✔
> palette
> technique
> armature ✔
> plate

1. an artwork made from materials glued to a flat surface
2. a material used for making art
3. the surface on which an image is created to make a print
4. the art and science of planning and drawing buildings
5. made by cutting or scratching an image into a surface
6. a way of working with media to make an artwork
7. a tray or board on which artists mix thick paints
8. a framework for a sculpture
9. an artwork made from cloth or fibers
10. a collage made from photographs

Artists and Their Art

B Each artwork listed in the box below appears in this unit. Use the titles to finish the sentences.

> *Landscape with Three Trees*
> *Guitar Player*
> *Bowl*
> *Stegosaurus*
> *Lam Tin Park, Lam Tin, Hong Kong*
> *Tapestry Weave Rag Jerga*

1. ___, by Freshman Brown, is a mixed-media artwork.
2. Leo Sewell's ___ is an example of sculpture in the round.
3. Rembrandt van Rijn used etching to show fine detail in ___.
4. Maria Montoya Martinez used the coil technique to make ___.
5. Agueda Martínez's ___ is a textile.
6. ___, by Ryan Li, is a photomontage.

Leo Sewell

Maria Montoya Martinez

Rembrandt van Rijn. *Portrait of the Artist in a Toque and Gold Chain,* 17th century.

Respond to Art

Romare Bearden. *Patchwork Quilt,* 1970. Cut-and-pasted cloth and paper with synthetic paint on composition board, 35 ³/₄ by 47 ⁷/₈ inches. The Museum of Modern Art, New York. © Estate of Romare Bearden/Licensed by VAGA, New York.

C **Look at *Patchwork Quilt* by Romare Bearden. Then match the letters in the line drawing of the collage to the art terms.**

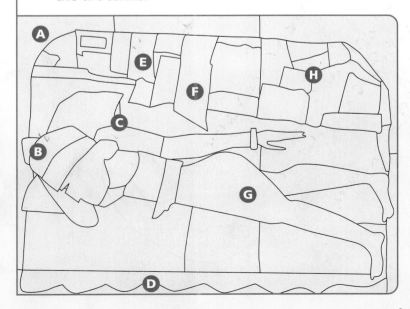

Art Terms

1. collage
2. mixed media
3. pattern
4. focal point
5. painting
6. variety
7. rhythm
8. textiles

Unit 3 *Review*

Write About Art

Short Story

D Look back at the artworks in this unit. Choose one that suggests a story to you. Copy the chart below and fill it in. Use the completed chart to help you write a short story inspired by the artwork you chose.

Name of Artwork

A. Main Character:

B. Secondary Character:

C. Setting:

D. Story Problem:

E. Beginning:

F. Middle:

G. End:

Your Studio Work

E Answer these questions in your Sketchbook Journal or on a separate sheet of paper.

1. What medium or technique in this unit interested you or challenged you the most? Explain.
2. What problems did you have as you worked with new media and techniques? How did you solve them? What will you do differently next time?
3. Which artworks inspired your own art-making process?
4. Choose one artwork to keep in your portfolio. Tell why you chose it.

Put It All Together

Sandy Skoglund. *Raining Popcorn*, 2001. Cibachrome print. Faulconer Gallery, Grinnell College. © 2001 Sandy Skoglund.

F Discuss or write about Skoglund's artwork *Raining Popcorn* using the four steps for critically viewing artwork.

1. **Describe** What does this artwork show? Describe the figures and objects and their environment.
2. **Analyze** What media and techniques did Skoglund use to create the artwork? What clues help you recognize them?
3. **Interpret** What do you think is the meaning or message of this artwork? What is the mood? What does it suggest about the artist's personality and attitudes?

4. **Judge** American artist Sandy Skoglund (1946–) calls the technique she used in *Raining Popcorn* tableau photography. A tableau is a staged, motionless scene. Skoglund hopes her tableaus will make viewers curious and inspire them to invent their own meanings and stories. Explain why you think Skoglund did or did not achieve her goals with this artwork.

"The more I do this kind of work, the more it feels like making a film. A film in one frame." —SANDY SKOGLUND

Artist Sandy Skoglund creates her artworks as scenes to be viewed live and then records them on film.

William H. Johnson. *Art Class,* ca. 1938–1939. Oil on plywood. Smithsonian American Art Museum, Washington, D.C.

The Creative Process

You can find **subjects** for artworks all around you, in any location, in any environment. Artworks may show a subject as simple as a leaf on a tree. Or the subject may be as detailed as the workings of a machine. Notice what William H. Johnson chose to show in his painting, *Art Class.* Many artists include subjects from the **human-made environment** in their artworks, such as buildings and cars. Other artists prefer to create artworks with trees and mountains from the **natural environment** as their subjects. If you were to draw what you see around you right now, would your subject be from the natural or human-made environment, or both?

As you explore the artworks in this unit, think about why each artist chose his or her subject. You will find that subjects for artworks are limitless. Consider how objects from both environments can help you express ideas in your artworks.

About *the Artist*

William H. Johnson began studying art at age seventeen. His subjects often included people and landscapes. At the age of forty, Johnson had his first solo exhibition in New York. Find out more about the artist's life and art on pages 172–173.

William H. Johnson. *Self-Portrait,* 1929.

Observing and Drawing

A first step when beginning to draw is observing the subject. An artist looks carefully at a subject before making the first line on the paper. Think about how the artist may have prepared to draw the subject shown in the drawing below. He probably first looked at the subject as a whole. Then he looked at the individual parts and how they relate to one another. He also likely looked at the subject from different angles before choosing which view to show.

Look closely at the drawing to notice the shading technique Eakins used, and the direction of the light source. The artist also used value and contrast to show the form of the machine. Notice the types of lines he included, and how the wheels show radial balance.

Thomas Eakins. *Perspective of a Lathe,* 1860. Pen, ink, and watercolor, 16 ⁵/₁₆ by 22 inches. Hirshhorn Museum and Sculpture Garden, Smithsonian Institution, Washington, D.C.

What would the artist need to study first in order to draw such a complex machine?

Titian Ramsey Peale. *The Gigantic Mastodon,* 1821. Ink wash, 14 by 19 inches. American Philosophical Society Library, Philidelphia, PA.

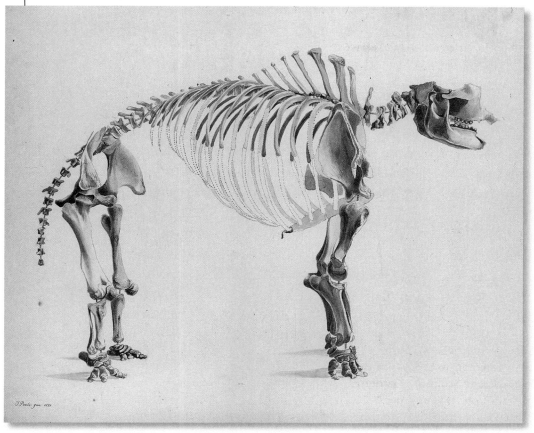

What do you think the artist learned about the extinct mastodon by drawing its skeleton?

Drawing to Understand

For artists, observing and drawing go hand in hand. Observing helps them draw, and drawing often helps them see and understand their subjects better. American artist Titian Ramsey Peale (1799–1881) observed a mastodon skeleton in a museum before making this drawing. Peale had never seen a living mastodon, of course. They had long been extinct. It was probably easier for him to imagine what a mastodon looked like after he made this drawing. He may have looked at the skeleton from different angles. He noticed how big each part was compared to other parts. As he drew the skeleton, he was able to visualize how the animal was put together.

Sketchbook Journal

Find an unusual human-made object, such as a tool or a simple machine. Choose an object that has several parts. Observe the object carefully. Then draw it from different points of view. Notice which drawing shows the object most clearly, and which one best shows the object's purpose.

Subject *Studies*

Pablo Picasso. *Study of a Horse for Guernica,* ca. 1937. Graphite on paper.

The drawing above by Spanish artist Pablo Picasso (1881–1973) is a **study,** or preparatory drawing. Picasso made the study to help him plan a larger, more complex artwork. Look for these details:

- The drawing is made with loose, simple lines to show the horse in an action pose, similar to a gesture drawing.
- The lines show parts of the horse in different poses.
- Bold lines indicate the artist's choice of poses and emphasize the horse's position and action.

Murals

The larger artwork for which Picasso drew this study is a mural titled *Guernica.* A **mural** is a large artwork that is often created directly on a wall or ceiling of a public building. Some murals, such as

Guernica, are created on canvas and displayed for public viewing. Most are painted, but other techniques may be used. Their subjects often reflect scenes, people, animals, and community or political events.

Technique Tip

Move the Artist

Studies often show subjects from different positions or angles. For large objects like a tree, you must move around them to see the different views. You can move small objects to new positions, but try moving the artist instead of the subject. Even for small objects, different backgrounds and the angle of light can reveal new views for drawing your subject.

Draw Studies to Plan a Mural

Use what you have learned about observing and drawing to draw studies for a community mural.

Materials

✓ 12" × 18" white drawing paper
✓ drawing media

1 Choose a subject for a mural to be displayed in your community. Decide what objects from the human-made and natural environments to include.

2 Draw studies from different angles or in different ways to discover how to show ideas about them.

3 Choose one of your study drawings to make a final drawing. Show how your subject or subjects would appear in your final mural design.

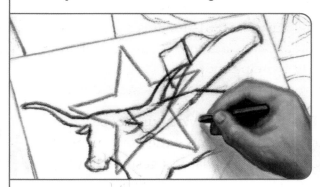

Review and Reflect

- What words best describe the subjects of your studies?
- How did you decide what angles or positions to use to show your subjects?
- What might a viewer infer from each study about the meaning of your mural?
- What do you like best and least about your studies? Explain.

People As Subjects

There are about six billion people on Earth, living, working, and playing. No two of them look exactly alike, have the same smile, or move in just the same way. Yet, every one of them is at least a little bit like you.

Every artwork that shows people reveals something about the human experience. Dutch artist Frans Hals (1580–1666) was fascinated with the expressive power of the human face. He spent most of his career capturing the features and personalities of the people he met. Look at Hals's portrait of Pieter van den Broecke. Notice how the colors of the subject's face hint at his career as a traveling merchant. His forehead appears lighter as if protected from the sun by a hat. What does the painting tell you about the subject's personality?

Frans Hals. *Pieter van den Broecke,* 1633. Oil on canvas. Kentwood, London.

How does this portrait help show the subject's career as a traveling merchant?

Margaret Burroughs. *Face of Africa*, ca.1965. Linocut, 11 ¹³/₁₆ by 10 inches. St. Louis Art Museum, St. Louis, MO. Museum Minority Artists Purchase Fund.

People and Their Stories

Just as each person has a unique face, each person has a unique story. Artworks that tell or suggest those stories are called **narrative** artworks. Look at the linocut print, *Face of Africa*, by African American artist Margaret Burroughs (1917–). Think about the ways in which the artwork visually tells the woman's story. What can you discover about her life from the background? What does her expression reveal? How does the medium the artist used influence your impression of the woman? All of these factors contribute to the narrative element of the artwork.

Sketchbook Journal

As you go through the day, observe the people around you with an artist's eye. Notice details about how people look, how they move, and how they interact with others. Draw people whom you find especially interesting. Make notes about how posture, motions, and expressions convey meaning.

People *and Gestures*

Diego Rivera. *Delfina Flores,* 1927. Oil on canvas, 32 by 26 inches. Marion Koogler McNay Art Museum, San Antonio, TX. Bequest of Marion Koogler McNay, 1950. 124.

How would you describe the girl based on her facial expression?

Artworks of people often reveal the subject's expressive qualities. Artists use a variety of techniques to help draw the viewer's eye to their subject. Look for these details in the portrait above by Mexican artist Diego Rivera (1886–1957):

- The young girl is placed in the center of the artwork, making her the focal point.
- The diagonal lines of the floor help lead your eye to the girl.
- The proportions of the girl's head and feet show that she is viewed from slightly above eye level.

Expressive Gestures

The solemn and timid expression of Delfina Flores is reflected in her face and body position and actions, or **gestures.** Her clenched hands help emphasize her appearance of shyness. Her hands appear to be playing nervously with the beads around her neck.

Rivera's murals and paintings often tell about cultural and political events, and everyday life. His artworks often show pairs or groups of people. The expressive gestures of the people he includes help tell the artwork's visual story. Think of ways that you can show the expressive qualities of people as subjects in your artworks.

Technique Tip

Proportions

Here are some proportions to use when drawing people:

- **Most adults are seven to eight times as tall as the length of their head.**
- **The center of the eyes is about halfway between the top of the head and the chin.**
- **The bottom of the nose is about halfway between the eyes and the chin.**

Draw a Group of People

Use what you have learned about people as subjects to draw a group of people.

Materials

- ✓ 12" × 18" sheets of newsprint
- ✓ black crayon or charcoal
- ✓ 12" × 18" sheets of white drawing paper
- ✓ colored markers or crayons

1 Have three classmates pose for you. Have them strike several poses as if in different settings, such as in class or at a sports event.

2 Use a black crayon or charcoal to draw the group. Capture positions and gestures more than facial details.

3 Select figures from different sketches. Use colored markers or crayons to redraw these figures in a new arrangement.

Review and Reflect

- Describe each of the groups in your drawings.
- How did your new arrangement unify your drawing?
- What narrative does your drawing suggest?
- Did you succeed in showing each person's emotions through gestures? Explain.

Self-Portraits

Have you ever held a camera at arm's length and snapped a picture or drawn a cartoon of yourself? If you have, you have made a **self-portrait.** Artists throughout time have made self-portraits using a variety of media. Some are painted, some are made in collage, and some are sculpted in stone.

For viewers, the most interesting thing about a self-portrait may be how an artist chooses to show himself or herself.

German artist Käthe Kollwitz (1867–1945) used lines and value to create this self-portrait at age sixty-seven. What do you think the portrait says about the artist?

Käthe Kollwitz. *Self-Portrait*, 1934. Lithograph on brown wove paper, 8 1/4 by 7 1/4 inches. National Gallery of Art, Washington, D.C.

Francesco Mazzola Parmigianino. *Self-Portrait in a Convex Mirror,* 1524. Oil on wood, diameter 9 ½ inches. Kunsthistorisches Museum, Vienna, Austria.

Self-Portraits and Self-Expression

A self-portrait is not always a true-to-life image of the artist. In the self-portrait above, Italian artist Parmigianino (1503–1540) showed how he looked in a convex mirror. A convex mirror is one whose surface curves outward like the side of a bubble. Why do you think Parmigianino used this type of mirror? How did the mirror change his appearance?

Artists express themselves in self-portraits through what they include or emphasize. Objects they show in the background can also give the viewer additional information about the artist.

Sketchbook Journal

Get acquainted with your face by drawing a close-up self-portrait. Hold a mirror close so that your face fills the whole mirror. Use a pencil to draw the shape of your face, filling the paper just as your face fills the mirror. Then observe your face carefully and draw your eyes, nose, mouth, and hairline.

Studio 3 Setup
Reflected *Self-Portraits*

M. C. Escher. *Hand With Reflecting Sphere,*
1935. Lithograph, 12 ½ by 8 ⅜ inches.

Based on this self-portrait, how would you describe
the artist?

In this self-portrait by Dutch artist M. C.
Escher (1898–1972), the artist made many
choices that influence how viewers see him.
Notice these details:

- The artist chose to show himself reflected
  in a sphere. Escher also chose to show
  his hand holding the sphere. All details
  appear within the sphere.

- The background, or negative space, of
  the print is empty, making the sphere
  and hand the focal point. His hand and
  the sphere fill the surface of the print.

What to Show

A technique used to omit items is
cropping, which involves trimming away
unwanted material or placing an edge on
the artwork so that only part of an object
can be seen. Each of the three self-portraits
in this lesson show examples of
cropping. The self-portrait by Kollwitz
shows where the drawing stops,
omitting any background. The mirrors
used by Parmigianino and Escher cropped
any unwanted background. The artists
chose their positions so that only the
desired objects would be reflected.

Technique Tip

Practice with Lighting

**The kind of light, the amount of
light, and the direction from which
the light comes all affect a self-
portrait. Practice studying your face
in a mirror with various kinds of
lighting. First stand next to a window.
Then stand in a dark room and hold
a flashlight in various positions, such
as under your chin and shining
down from above your head.**

Studio 3

Draw a Self-Portrait

Use what you have learned to draw a self-portrait.

Materials

- ✓ reflective sphere or ornament
- ✓ lamp or other light source
- ✓ 12" × 18" drawing paper
- ✓ pencil
- ✓ colored pencils or oil pastels

1 Holding the reflective object, position the light source to cast an interesting reflection of your face.

2 Observe your reflection and notice how it affects your features. Use a pencil to draw your self-portrait.

3 Use colored pencils or oil pastels to complete your self-portrait.

Review and Reflect

- Describe the special features in your self-portrait as it is reflected.
- How did you use light to affect your reflection?
- What do the colors and shading you used show about your personality?
- What, if anything, would you change about your self-portrait? Explain.

Lesson 4

Subjects in Still Life

Artists have been arranging food, flowers, books, and other common items as subjects of **still lifes** for thousands of years. The still lifes on this page show objects that were common to the period in which they were painted. Artists pay careful attention to the arrangement of objects before they begin to paint. The arrangement of objects in these paintings creates asymmetrical balance. Each artist's use of value and shading creates the illusion of space and depth.

The subjects of still lifes may also include a variety of shapes, forms, patterns, and textures. Some artists choose subjects that reflect his or her interests or personality. Combinations such as these can add unity, variety, and interest. No matter the subject, a still life provides a sense of present moment.

How did this Roman artist create a convincing illusion of three-dimensional objects?

Artist unknown, Roman. *Glass Bowl With Fruit,* 1st century. Wall painting. National Archaeological Museum, Naples, Italy.

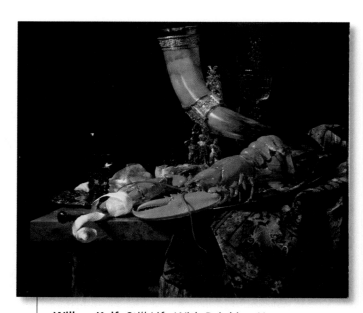

Willem Kalf. *Still Life With Drinking Horn,* ca. 1653. Oil on canvas, 34 by 40 ¼ inches. National Gallery, London.

Arthur Dove. *The Lobster,* 1908. Oil on canvas, 25 7/8 by 32 inches. Amon Carter Museum, Fort Worth, TX.

Appeal to the Senses

Many still lifes are arranged and painted to appeal to the viewer's senses. This still life by American artist Arthur Dove (1880–1946) is an example of such a still life. The artist chose foods that many people enjoy. Lobster and fruit also have lively and tangy tastes that viewers may know. The vibrant red of the lobster makes it the focal point. Dove's use of flowers in the background and on the pitcher creates unity. The thick, heavy brushstrokes create texture. Notice how the objects are defined by dark outlines and colorful shadows. The contrast between the warm and cool colors adds variety. How would you describe Dove's style? Why?

Blooming *Still Lifes*

Artist unknown. *Tree Peonies, Garden Rocks and Insects,* ca. 13th–14th century. Hanging scroll, ink and color on silk, 76 ½ by 41 ⅛ inches. Nelson-Atkins Museum of Art, Kansas City, MO, gift of Bronson Trevor in honor of his father, John B. Trevor, 76–10/7A.

What effect does the dark background have in this still life?

People in all parts of the world value flowers for their beauty and fragrance. This universal appeal makes flowers a favorite subject for still-life artworks. The still life above was made by an unknown Chinese artist several centuries ago. Yet it appeals to viewers now as much as it did then. Notice these details:

- The artist emphasized the blooms of the flowers by using contrast to draw the viewer's attention.
- The artist also painted the blooms in detail. He or she showed their many layers of soft petals. The visual texture suggests the delicacy of real flowers.

Still-Life Styles

The art of Chinese scroll painting dates back to the fourth century A.D. The early scrolls were created to teach religious lessons. They later evolved into rich landscapes, drawing the viewer's eye into the artwork. Many still-life artworks like this hanging scroll show their subjects in realistic detail. But some artists choose different techniques, color schemes, and styles. They may combine a variety of media or use a monochromatic color scheme. How might this still life be different if the artist had used only geometric shapes?

Technique Tip

Oil Pastels

Oil pastels are similar to crayons. You can achieve different effects depending on how hard you press as you draw. Oil pastels also allow you to blend colors. Apply two colors side by side, and then blend one into the other with your finger. Also try applying one color over another and blending to create a new color.

Studio 4

Draw a Still Life

Use what you have learned about still lifes to draw a still-life arrangement of plants or flowers.

Materials

- ✓ arrangement of flowers or plant cuttings in a container
- ✓ newsprint
- ✓ pencil
- ✓ colored pencils
- ✓ 12" × 18" dark-colored construction paper
- ✓ oil pastels

1 Observe the arrangement carefully. Then use a pencil to make sketches of it on newsprint.

2 Use a light-colored pencil to draw the arrangement on dark-colored paper. Include detail, but use only lines.

3 Use oil pastels to complete the focal points of your still life. Use colors close to the color of the paper to show depth.

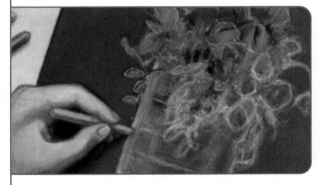

Review and Reflect

- Describe the arrangement of the plants or flowers in your still life.
- How do the colors you used create a focal point?
- What feeling or mood did you intend your still life to convey? How do the colors you used contribute to that mood?
- How might you approach another still life using the same materials?

Meet *the Artist*

William H. Johnson

William H. Johnson was born into a poor family in the American South. In spite of humble beginnings and racial prejudices, Johnson succeeded as an artist. He lived for a time in Europe. There, he was influenced by the art of French artists Paul Cézanne and Chaim Soutine. Johnson developed his own style of brightly colored paintings with simple forms. More than a thousand of his paintings are now in the Smithsonian American Art Museum. People were his favorite subjects.

William H. Johnson. *Self-Portrait,* 1929. Oil on canvas, 23 ¼ by 18 ¼ inches. Smithsonian American Art Museum, Washington, D.C.

"My aim is to express in a natural way what I feel, what is in me, both rhythmically and spiritually. . ."

—WILLIAM H. JOHNSON

Johnson painted portraits of soldiers, past presidents, and his family.

Student Days

When he was seventeen years old, William H. Johnson left his home in South Carolina and moved to New York City. He knew he wanted to be an artist. As an African American, Johnson also knew that he would not find much opportunity in the South. Racial prejudice was still all too common.

Soon after arriving in New York, Johnson entered the National Academy of Design. His painting skills won him several awards at the academy. When he graduated, one of his teachers raised money for him to live and study art in France.

Success in the United States

Johnson lived in Europe for more than ten years. He traveled widely, painting and showing his work from Scandinavia to North Africa. In 1938, Johnson returned to the United States. He became an art teacher in New York's Harlem area. Harlem was a center of African American art, music, dance, and literature. Johnson began to paint portraits of people enjoying Harlem's lively life. A New York gallery held the first solo exhibition of Johnson's artworks in 1941. Except for brief periods in South Carolina and Norway, Johnson spent the rest of his life in New York, where he died in 1970.

Talk About It

- Do you think Johnson might have been a good art teacher? Explain.

- Why might artists like William H. Johnson want to study and create artworks in different parts of the world?

The Life of William H. Johnson

1900

1901
William H. Johnson born in Florence, South Carolina (March 18)

New York City, 1918

Johnson goes to New York City
1918

Johnson accepted as a student at the National Academy of Design

1920

1921

Eiffel Tower, Paris, France

1926
Johnson travels to Paris, where he is influenced by French artists

1939
Back in New York, Johnson teaches art

1940

1941
First solo exhibition of Johnson's artworks in New York

1944
Johnson moves back to his hometown for a short time

Smithsonian American Art Museum

Smithsonian American Art Museum (then known as The National Museum of American Art) acquires more than one thousand of Johnson's artworks

1960

1967

1970
Johnson dies on Long Island, New York, April 13

1980

Look *and Compare*

Still Life in Two Styles

William H. Johnson painted a variety of subjects, such as people, landscapes, and historical events. He also experimented with still lifes as subjects. Like Johnson, Carolyn Brady has experimented with different subjects, including landscapes. Her favorite subject, however, is a still life. Her still lifes are often referred to as "tablescapes."

Common objects can become subjects of still lifes.

An Expressive Still Life

William H. Johnson once wrote, "I am not afraid to exaggerate a contour, a form, or anything that gives more character and movement to the canvas." Johnson did not try to paint his subjects in realistic detail. Instead, he used lines, shapes, and colors to express important qualities about the subjects. Notice how Johnson simplified the objects and repeated colors in *Still Life— Fruit, Bottles.* Where do you notice exaggerated forms? Do you agree with the artist that the exaggerated forms give "more character and movement to the canvas"? Why or why not?

A Realistic Still Life

After earning a master's degree in fine art, American artist Carolyn Brady (1937–) worked for a textile design studio. There she used watercolor to create designs for fabrics. She worked to develop her understanding of the medium. Today, she chooses to work only in watercolor. Brady uses the medium to paint her subjects in realistic detail. The viewer can almost smell the flowers in her still life, *Delphiniums and Roses on Glass.* The greenery in the background gives the illusion of space and depth. Notice how the colors and textures add to the painting's realistic qualities.

Compare the glass bottles in Johnson's painting to the glass objects in Brady's still life. Each artist used his or her own special style to show similar objects. What do you think Johnson might say about the realism of Brady's painting? Why do you think so?

William H. Johnson. *Still Life—Fruit, Bottles,* ca. 1938–1939. Oil on burlap, 21 ⅛ by 32 ⅛ inches. Smithsonian American Art Museum, Washington, D.C.

Carolyn Brady. *Delphiniums and Roses on Glass,* 1985. Watercolor on paper, 60 by 40 inches. Nancy Hoffman Gallery, New York.

Compare & Contrast

- Describe the similarities in these two paintings. How does each artist's use of the elements of art differ?

- Which still life appeals to you more? Explain.

Animals As Subjects

Some of the oldest known paintings are of animals. Prehistoric paintings on the walls of a cave in France show bison and horses, and are more than thirty thousand years old. When they were painted, people needed animals for food, clothing, tools, and weapons. Animals are not the means by which most people live today, but they remain a common and popular subject for artworks.

Italian-born American artist John Singer Sargent (1856–1925) is known for his portraits. He was often paid very well to paint portraits of wealthy European society. About 1910, Sargent changed from oil paints to watercolors as his medium. The subjects of his artworks also changed. He used tints and shades of the watercolor to capture the form and texture of the animals in the painting below.

John Singer Sargent. *Muddy Alligators,* 1917. Watercolor, 13 9/16 by 20 15/16 inches. Worcester Art Museum, Worcester, MA.

How has Sargent suggested the rough texture of the alligators' skin?

John James Audubon. *Brown or Norway Rat,*
1848. Pencil and watercolor, 24 by 32 ⅝ inches.
Pierpont Morgan Library, New York.

Light pencil lines and the positions of the rats
give the illusion of form to the melon on which
the rats are feeding.

Animals in Nature

American naturalist John James Audubon
(1785–1851) is also known as a wildlife
artist. His drawings of birds and four-legged
animals grace the pages of several books,
including *The Birds of North America.* His
observations and views of nature helped
make people more aware of the need to
protect the feathered creatures. Audubon
spent years studying the animals he drew.
He learned about their bodies and how they
moved. *Brown or Norway Rat* shows all but
one of the animals in **profile,** or side view.
Notice how the artist used value in this view
to show texture and the animals' muscle
structure.

John James Audubon. *Blue Jay,* 1825. India ink and
watercolor, 23 by 18 ⅞ inches. New York Historical
Society, New York.

Sketchbook Journal

**Observe domestic animals or
those in a local zoo. Notice the
location of each animal's eyes.
Do they face forward or are
they on the sides of the
animal's head? Also watch how
the animals move. Then make
sketches of different animals in
a variety of positions. Note any
similarities and differences.**

Studio 5 Setup
Animals *in Sculpture*

Yuyu Yang (also known as Yang Ying-feng).
Advent of the Phoenix, 1970. Stainless steel,
height 23 feet. Osaka, Japan.

How did the artist give the illusion of movement in
this sculpture?

Chinese artist Yuyu Yang (1926–1997) was often inspired by the harmony between humans and nature. *Advent of the Phoenix* shows Yang's impression of a legendary bird. Look for these details in the sculpture:

- The larger-than-life bird is made up of curved geometric forms.
- The hole representing the bird's eye creates negative space.
- The artist's use of stainless steel gives the sculpture a smooth, shiny texture.

Abstract Symbols

Symbolic animals have appeared in artworks throughout history. The phoenix is a mythological bird attributed to the ancient Egyptians. It was associated with the worship of the sun. In Chinese culture, the phoenix is a symbol of the empress and of beauty. How does *Advent of the Phoenix* reflect the Chinese symbol?

Abstract artworks, such as Yang's sculpture, do not show the subject in a realistic way. Although it is abstract, the viewer can still interpret the sculpture as being a bird. The five curved forms give the illusion of motion, similar to a bird in flight. Abstract artists often use bold colors and geometric shapes and forms to simplify their subjects. In some abstract artworks, the subject is not recognizable at all.

Technique Tip

Armatures
You can use newspaper and cardboard to make an armature or frame for an animal sculpture. Roll newspaper into cylinders and tape them to make legs or torsos. Fold cardboard into cones, cubes, and other forms for other body parts. Glue or tape the forms together to make the armature.

Studio 5

Make a Papier-Mâché Insect

Use what you have learned about animals as subjects to make an imaginary papier-mâché insect.

Materials

- ✓ 12" × 18" newsprint and a pencil
- ✓ newspapers and cardboard scraps
- ✓ scissors ⓢ
- ✓ masking tape
- ✓ papier-mâché paste
- ✓ newspaper or paper towel strips
- ✓ tempera or acrylic paints, brushes, and water
- ✓ yarn, beads, and other found objects

1 Make sketches of a design for your insect sculpture. Show the insect from each side. Then make the armature.

2 Apply paper strips using papier-mâché paste. Smooth each strip, or use the creases and wrinkles as part of your insect's texture. Allow to dry.

3 Paint your sculpture and then add features and details.

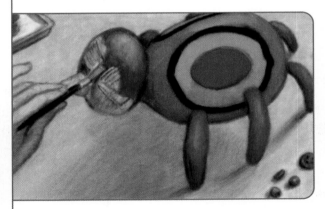

Review and Reflect

- Describe the parts of your imaginary insect.
- How do the proportions of your sculpture compare with those of an actual insect?
- What qualities of your insect make it interesting to viewers?
- What do you enjoy most and least about working with papier mâché? Why?

Lesson 6

Landscapes As Subjects

Artists who love nature and the outdoors often draw or paint landscapes. These artworks show natural environments, such as mountains and sky, rivers and forests. Landscape artworks vary as much as nature itself. They may show a glowing sunrise, as in the painting below, or a howling blizzard.

Some artists choose to paint a **panorama,** or wide view, in the natural environment. Others prefer to rely on their imaginations. Do you think Frederic Church (1826–1900) painted *The River of Light* from observation or from his imagination? Why do you think so?

What technique did the artist use to show space and depth in this painting?

Frederic Church. *The River of Light,* 1877. Oil on canvas, 54 3/8 by 84 1/8 inches. National Gallery of Art, Washington, D.C.

Gabriele Münter. *Staffelsee in Autumn,* 1923. Oil on board, 13 ¾ by 19 ¼ inches. The National Museum of Women in the Arts, Washington, D.C., gift of Wallace and Wilhelmina Holladay. ©Artists Rights Society (ARS), New York/VG Bild-Kunst, Bonn.

This painting shows a panorama of a German countryside.

Scale and Placement

Views of the Staffelsee countryside offered German artist Gabriele Münter (1877–1962) a variety of subjects. The landscape painting above shows her style of using vibrant colors and bold brushstrokes. She used the scale and placement of objects and figures to show space and depth. What do you notice about the lamb in the foreground in relation to the figure moving down the hill? Münter's use of overlapping adds to the illusion of space. The houses overlap some of the trees and the lake, making them appear closer. How do these techniques compare with Frederic Church's use of atmospheric perspective to show space and depth in *The River of Light?*

Sketchbook Journal

Make sketches of the sky at different times of day. Note the way the colors in the sky change throughout the day, from sunrise to late morning, midday, afternoon, and sunset. Observe a sunset closely. Watch how colors in the sky change and how this affects the colors of objects on Earth.

Expressive *Landscapes*

Robert Scott Duncanson. *Valley Pasture*, 1857. Oil on canvas, 32 by 48 inches. Smithsonian American Art Museum, Washington, D.C.

What time of day is shown in this painting? How can you tell?

Artists who create landscapes want viewers to see more than just land and sky. They try to suggest a feeling that viewers might have if they could actually visit the scene in the artwork. Look for these details in this landscape by African American artist Robert Scott Duncanson (1821–1872):

- The organic shapes of the rolling hills draw the viewer's eye to the lake. Two figures stand at the edge of the water with a boat, perhaps going or returning from fishing.
- The lake appears calm and serene as it reflects the blues of the sky and colors of the hills. Sheep and cattle are grazing nearby.
- A second lake appears in the distance, leading the viewer further into the painting.

Mood in Landscape

Duncanson expressed a calm and serene mood by showing a peaceful landscape at a particular time of day. The soft color palette adds to the warmth of the painting. Would the mood of this landscape be different if Duncanson had painted it showing a different season and time of day? Explain.

Technique Tip

Highlights

You can use an eraser to remove color and create highlights when using chalk pastels. This technique can be especially helpful when drawing landscapes. For example, erasing color can help you show clouds or spray created by waterfalls. Also, erasing selected parts of plants and other objects can show areas of bright sunlight.

Draw a Landscape

Use what you have learned about landscapes as subjects to draw a landscape.

Materials

✓ notebook paper
✓ pencil
✓ 12" × 18" drawing paper
✓ chalk pastels or colored pencils

1 Write these words on a sheet of paper, leaving space beneath each one: *desert, glacier, meadow, forest, island.* Write five words that describe each place.

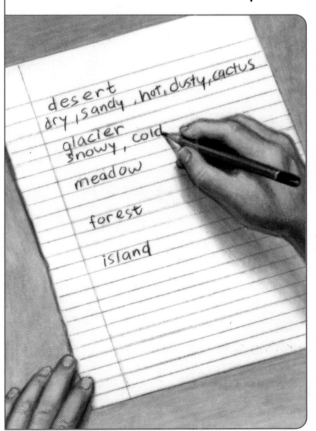

2 Choose and draw one place as the subject of a landscape. Let the five words guide your choice of objects, colors, and textures to include.

3 Add color, texture, and details. Include techniques you have learned to show space and depth.

Review and Reflect

- Describe the sights, sounds, smells, and textures of the place you drew.
- Why did you include the objects that you did? How do the colors you chose contribute to your landscape?
- What is the mood of your landscape? What would be a good title for it?
- Does your landscape show a place that you would like to visit? Explain.

Lesson 7

Seascapes As Subjects

A **seascape** is an artwork with the sea as its subject, or one in which the sea plays an important part. The most well-known seascape artists have lived near the sea and spent their lives observing it. Humans have feared and been fascinated by the sea, and artists have long worked to capture its beauty and power. Whether it shows a single wave or a vast expanse of ocean, a seascape can draw viewers into the mystery of the sea.

Katsushika Hokusai. *The Great Wave Off Kanagawa,* 1823–1829. Colored woodcut, 10 1/8 by 15 inches. Metropolitan Museum of Art, New York.

What natural object provides a contrast to the violence of the waves?

Winslow Homer. *Gloucester Harbor,* 1873.
Oil on canvas, 15 9/16 by 22 7/16 inches.
Nelson-Atkins Museum of Art, Kansas City, MO.

What mood do the warm colors of the sunset convey?

A Sea of Contrasts

An artist could observe the oceans for a lifetime and never run out of new ideas for artworks. The seascapes on these pages show both the turbulence and serenity of the water. Notice how Japanese artist Katsushika Hokusai (1760–1849) contrasted the rhythm of the waves with a serene view of Mount Fuji in the background. American artist Winslow Homer (1836–1910) painted other subjects, but he specialized in seascapes. Born in the seaport city of Boston, he created realistic images of the sea. Homer used oils and watercolors to capture the colors and beauty of a calm sea in the northern light.

Research

Do research to learn more about seascapes. Focus your research on visual resources. Find as many examples as you can of seascapes that have been created at different times and places. Analyze each one and make notes about the similarities and differences. How might you apply your findings to your artworks?

Bernard Stanley Hoyes.
Cool Runnings, 1990.
Oil on canvas, 24 by 36 inches.
Collection of the artist.
© Bernard Stanley Hoyes.

How did the artist create
the illusion that the viewer
is part of the scene?

Bernard Stanley Hoyes (1951–) often uses symbols of his native culture in his artworks. Hoyes is an American artist, but he was not born in the United States. Look for clues about his heritage in the painting above. Then notice these details:

- Look closely at the colors of the water. Notice how Hoyes showed where the water is shallow and where it is deeper, as well as how he painted the breakers rolling into shore.
- Notice other colors in the painting. They are warm and bright, reflecting a tropical climate.
- The color and detail of the bird on the branch give the illusion that the viewer is observing the scene from under a tree.

Seeing the Sea

Water takes on the colors around it. In Hoyes's native Jamaica, it reflects the clear blue of the sky and the warm yellow tones of the strong sunlight. In Homer's painting of Gloucester, Massachusetts, the sea is colored by the dark sky and the weaker northern sunlight. Consider how the colors of the water add to the mood of each artwork.

Technique Tip

Watercolors

Watercolors have a transparent, fluid look that makes them a good medium for painting seascapes. You can make tints of a color by adding increasing amounts of water. The more water you add, the more transparent the paint will be. Practice making varied tints of blues and greens to achieve watery effects.

Studio 7

Paint a Seascape

Use what you have learned about seascapes as subjects to paint one that reflects a mood.

Materials

- ✓ sketchpad
- ✓ pencil
- ✓ watercolor paper
- ✓ crayons
- ✓ watercolors
- ✓ brushes and water container

1 Make several sketches of seascapes. Think about the location of each one and about the mood or feeling it could express.

2 Choose one sketch to paint. Lightly draw it on white paper. Apply white or light-colored crayon heavily on wave crests or light areas.

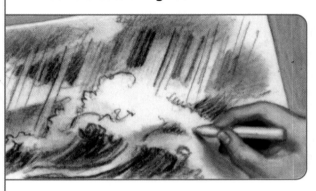

3 Use watercolors to paint your seascape. The crayon areas will resist the paint. Add contrast and detail with watercolor.

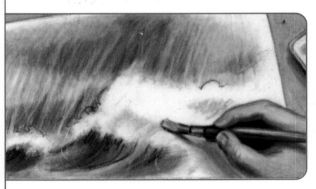

Review and Reflect

- Describe the setting and action of your seascape.
- How did you use the crayon resist and watercolors to show depth and contrast?
- What mood does your seascape reflect? How do the colors reflect the mood?
- What would you do next time to improve your seascape?

Lesson 8
Cityscapes As Subjects

A city is an ever-changing collage of colors, forms, lines, shapes, and textures. No wonder many artists are fascinated with showing the urban skylines in cityscapes. Artists have many position choices, or **points of view,** from which to show urban life. Some may show tops of buildings, bridges, and trees from a **bird's-eye view.** Other artists may show a brightly lit city at night from eye level in a **straight-on view.**

Ray Strong. *San Francisco from Russian Hill,* ca. 1933–1934. Oil on canvas, 30 by 40 ⅛ inches. Smithsonian American Art Museum, Washington, D.C.

Beulah Bettersworth. *Christopher Street, Greenwich Village,* 1934. Smithsonian American Art Museum, Washington, D.C.

City Streets

An artist's eye can frame many cityscapes in a single city. American artist Beulah Bettersworth (1894–1968) painted this view of a street in New York City. Think about where she was as she composed the artwork. Did she have a straight-on view or a bird's-eye view?

Bettersworth carefully chose her view of the street to create an interesting scene. The building in the center with an orange glow in its window is the focal point. The tire tracks in the road are parallel to the rows of buildings on either side. The lines of the tracks and the buildings lead the viewer's eye to the focal point.

Visual Culture

Watch for cityscapes that appear in various media. Television shows often open with them. Newspapers, magazine ads, and movies often show cityscapes. For each one, identify the point of view from which it was shown. Notice what mood or idea it conveys.

Views *of a City*

Gustave Caillebotte. *Snow on Roofs,* 1878. Musée d'Orsay, Paris.

How would this painting be different if it showed the city during spring or summer?

This wintry cityscape by French artist Gustave Caillebotte (1848–1894) shows the view of a city from a rooftop. Notice these details:

- The winter season depicted helps provide interest. The white snow provides contrast to the dark buildings and calls attention to repeated shapes.
- The bare trees in winter allow the rooftops and distant buildings to be visible.
- By including several rooftops, Caillebotte created a pattern. The regularity of the rooftops provides a sense of unity and harmony.

Mood in Cityscapes

The snow and the lack of activity in this cityscape suggest a peaceful calm. Compare this mood to that of Bettersworth's painting on page 189. It also shows a snowy city, but the bustle of people and the glowing lights in the windows add energy and warmth. What mood would you like to express in a cityscape? How will you express it?

Technique Tip

Working with Oil Pastels

You can blend colors when using oil pastels. Go over an area very lightly with the first color. Then go over the same area again, also very lightly, with another color. If you warm the oil pastels in your hand, the colors will go on more smoothly.

Draw a Cityscape

Use what you have learned about cityscapes to draw a city at night from a bird's-eye or straight-on view.

Materials

- ✓ sketchpad
- ✓ pencil
- ✓ 12" × 18" black or dark blue construction paper
- ✓ oil pastels or other color media

1 Choose a point of view from which to draw a real or imagined cityscape. You might imagine yourself in a hot-air balloon, or as a cat on a corner.

2 Make a sketch of your cityscape. Choose a mood or personal experience to express in your cityscape.

3 Transfer your sketch to the construction paper. Use oil pastels to complete your cityscape and reflect the mood.

Review and Reflect

- Describe the objects you included in your cityscape. What season did you show?
- What point of view did you choose for your cityscape? How did you show it?
- What mood and meaning does your cityscape convey?
- If you were to draw this cityscape again, what would you add or remove? Why?

Portfolio *Project*

Paint a Textured Still Life

Paul Cézanne. *Sugar Pot, Pears and Cloth,* ca. 1893. Oil on canvas, 20 by 24 inches. Private collection.

Plan

Look back at the still-life artworks shown in Lesson 4 and in the Look and Compare feature on page 175. Think about the different techniques the artists used to create these paintings and the effects they achieved. Then look closely at the still life above, which was painted by French artist Paul Cézanne (1839–1906).

- What technique did Cézanne use when he painted this still life? Look for brushstrokes and notice how they create texture in the background and table.
- In what areas are the brushstrokes most noticeable? What do you think Cézanne wanted to express about those areas?
- How could you use Cézanne's technique in a still life? What could you express by using thick paint to create texture?

Using what you have learned about still lifes, create your own still-life painting to show texture.

Sketchbook Journal

Choose objects to arrange for a still life. Select objects that have interesting shapes and colors rather than objects with many small details. Practice drawing each object without using solid lines. For example, use the side of a piece of charcoal to create the basic shapes of the objects.

Materials

- ✓ 12" × 18" white painting paper
- ✓ acrylic paints
- ✓ palette
- ✓ palette knife or cardboard strips

Create

1 Arrange the personal objects you have chosen for your still life.

2 Select a color scheme. Use a palette knife to mix the colors you will use in your painting.

3 Use a clean palette knife or a small strip of cardboard to paint the basic shapes in your still life.

4 Use a palette knife or cardboard strip to complete your still life. Apply paint thickly to create textures and to express your ideas about your subject.

Reflect

- What problems did you have while completing your still life? How did you solve them?
- How did you use texture to help you express an idea or a feeling?
- What did you learn about the techniques you used?
- Talk to a classmate about the project. How are your paintings the same? How are they different?

Unit 4 *Review*

Vocabulary Review

A Match each art term below with its definition.

> study   cropping
> profile   panorama
> mural   point of view
> human-made   gesture
>   environment   abstract
> subject

1. leaving out certain areas or objects to emphasize the ones shown
2. a large artwork that is often created directly on a wall or ceiling
3. what an artwork shows or what it is about
4. a side view
5. having a simplified, sometimes unrecognizable, subject
6. angle from which a subject is seen
7. drawing made to prepare for a larger, more complex artwork
8. surroundings with objects created by people
9. a view of a large area
10. body position or action

Artists and Their Art

B Each artwork listed in the box appears in this unit. Use the titles to finish the sentences.

> *Hand With Reflecting Sphere*
> *Advent of the Phoenix*
> *Valley Pasture*
> *Art Class*
> *Face of Africa*
> *Cool Runnings*
> *Christopher Street, Greenwich Village*
> *Staffelsee in Autumn*

1. ___, by Robert Scott Duncanson, shows a panorama.
2. Gabriele Münter used scale and placement in ___.
3. The subject of ___, by Yuyu Yang, is a legendary bird.
4. Beulah Bettersworth chose a snowy cityscape as her subject in___.
5. M. C. Escher's ___ is a self-portrait.
6. ___, by Bernard Stanley Hoyes, is a seascape painting.
7. ___ is a narrative linocut print by Margaret Burroughs.
8. ___, by William H. Johnson, shows a human-made environment.

Käthe Kollwitz

John James Audubon

Respond to Art

C **Look at *Cape Martin* by Monet. In a class discussion or on a sheet of paper, match each art term below with examples from the painting.**

Claude Monet. *Cape Martin,* also called *Marine,* 1884. Oil on canvas. Musée des Beaux-Arts, Tournai, Belgium.

Art Terms

1. seascape
2. tint
3. natural environment
4. texture
5. point of view
6. contrast
7. horizon line
8. visual rhythm

Unit 4 *Review*

Write About Art

Analyze an Artwork

D Look back at the artworks in this unit. Choose one that you think is especially interesting. Take time to observe the artwork. Consider the process the artist used to create it. For example, ask yourself questions such as these:

- Why did the artist choose this medium and point of view?
- What feelings and ideas did the artist hope to express about the subject? What techniques did he or she use to achieve this?

Write an essay giving your answers to these questions and reasons for your conclusions.

Your Studio Work

E Answer these questions in your Sketchbook Journal or on a separate sheet of paper.

1. What subject in this unit interested you the most? Explain.
2. What problems did you have as you experimented with each subject? How did you solve them? What will you do differently next time?
3. Which artworks inspired your own art-making process?
4. Choose one artwork to keep in your portfolio. Tell why you chose it.

Artwork Title

subject:
medium:
point of view:
feelings and ideas expressed:
techniques used:

Put It All Together

Suzi Gablik. *Tropism "12"*, 1972. Oil and photomechanical reproduction on canvas, 24 by 24 inches. Smithsonian American Art Museum, Washington, D.C.

F **Discuss or write about Gablik's artwork using the four steps for critically viewing artwork.**

1. **Describe** What is the subject of this artwork? Describe the figures and objects and their environment.
2. **Analyze** What point of view did Gablik use? What media and techniques did she use to create the artwork? What clues help you figure this out?
3. **Interpret** What do you think is the meaning or message of this artwork? What is the mood? What do you think *Tropism "12"* is about?
4. **Judge** American artist Suzi Gablik (1934–) has written that she wants her art to inspire people to appreciate the natural world. Do you think this artwork achieves the artist's desire? Explain.

In addition to being an artist, Suzi Gablik is a writer and teacher.

"At a time when other girls' minds were filled with boys, proms, and football games, my closest friends were [artists] Robert Rauschenberg and Jasper Johns." —SUZI GABLIK

Artist unknown, Mesopotamian. (Detail) *The Standard of Ur,* ca. 2500 B.C. Wood, lapis lazuli, and shell, length 19 inches. The British Museum, London.

Unit 5

Styles in Art History

For thousands of years, artists all over the world have expressed thoughts and feelings in artworks. They have developed media and techniques to show their ideas, their lives, their dreams, and their hopes and fears. Archaeologists and art historians have learned much of what we know about ancient people and cultures by studying their artworks. Buildings, sculptures, jewelry, paintings, coins, and pottery help tell about ancient life and civilizations. What does the artwork on page 198 tell you about life in ancient Mesopotamia?

Today's artists enrich their own artworks by studying the art styles of other artists and cultures. In this unit, you will explore artworks from Western European civilizations and North America. Many of their traditions began in ancient Greece and Rome. You will also learn about the art of Asia, Africa, and other regions. Get ready to discover what you have in common with artists from long ago and many places.

Artist unknown, Mesopotamian. *Gudea, King of Lagash,* 2120 B.C.

About *the Artist*

Mesopotamia means "the land between two rivers." The name refers to the plain between the Tigris and Euphrates rivers in present-day Iraq. You will learn more about Mesopotamia and its art styles on pages 204–207 and 220–223.

Prehistoric Styles

People began to communicate through artworks thousands of years before they began to write. The oldest known artworks are from the **Paleolithic** period, or Old Stone Age. Rock carvings found in caves near Cape Town, South Africa, show that humans have created artworks for more than seventy thousand years.

Prehistoric art, such as *Spotted Horses and Handprints,* was made before the start of written history. During this time, humans were hunters and gatherers. Animals were an important source of food. Their paintings often show horses, bison, and cattle. Cave paintings such as this may reflect a hunting event or ceremony. The stenciled handprints were likely made by blowing soot through a reed over a hand placed on the wall.

How do you think the spots on the horses were made?

Artist unknown, Paleolithic. *Spotted Horses and Handprints,* 15,000–10,000 B.C. Pech-Merle Caves, Lot, France.

Artist unknown, Neolithic. *Beaker with Ibex Design,* ca. 4000 B.C. Terra cotta, height 11 inches. Musée du Louvre, Paris.

What purpose could the artist have had for exaggerating the shapes of the animals?

A Giant Step Forward

The **Mesolithic** period, or Middle Stone Age (ca. 10,000–8000 B.C.), followed the Paleolithic period. Humans began to wander less and establish villages. Paintings and carvings from this period include human figures as well as animals.

By the New Stone Age, or **Neolithic** period (ca. 8000–3000 B.C.), humans were living in village-like communities. They were growing their own food and had domesticated animals. These early humans also developed functional artworks, such as pottery and weaving. The cup or beaker shown above shows how these artists also included animals in their designs. Objects such as this were likely used to hold food or water. Notice the artist's use of geometric lines and shapes. The artist used these elements to exaggerate the proportions of the animals.

Sketchbook Journal

Look closely at the simple shapes of the animals in the artwork. Then make your own simple sketches of animals, such as horses, lions, elephants, monkeys, and birds. Finally, draw some useful objects that you could decorate with these drawings.

Prehistoric *Murals*

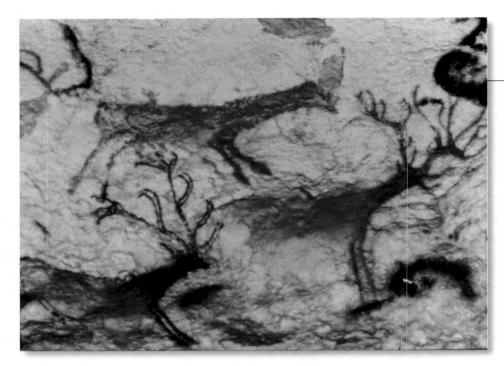

Artist unknown, Paleolithic. *Group of Stags,* ca. 18,000 B.C. Lascaux Caves, Perigord, Dordogne, France.

Why do you think ancient artists so often painted animals?

As you have read, some of the oldest known artworks were created during the Paleolithic period. The walls of this cave in France are covered with hundreds of such paintings. Notice these details:

- The animals are shown in profile. The profile view makes the animals easily recognizable. Perhaps this view was the one most familiar to the artist.
- The stags are shown as solid areas of color with no outlines. The artist used darker values of pigment in some areas.

Expression in Early Artworks

Unfortunately, no one knows for sure what these early artists wanted to express in these paintings. Perhaps they told a story about a hunting trip. Perhaps they are a symbol of humans' connection to nature. The body positions of the stags reflect the artist's observation of the animals; they appear to be in motion. Notice the types of lines the artist used to show the detail of the animals' antlers.

Technique Tip

"Prehistoric" Media

The cave artist used pigments or other media that could make thick lines on the uneven surfaces of cave walls. Some media were probably a little like oil pastels. Early artists also used charcoal. Experiment to see how different media work on a rock surface.

Studio 1

Create a Mural of Prehistoric Times

Use what you have learned about prehistoric art to create a mural.

Materials

- ✓ 30" × 60" brown craft paper
- ✓ black watercolor
- ✓ charcoal
- ✓ oil pastels in earth colors

1 With one or two classmates, wrinkle the paper and then stain it with a light wash of black watercolor. Let it dry completely.

2 Use charcoal to draw animals on the paper in a prehistoric style. Fill in some details with oil pastels.

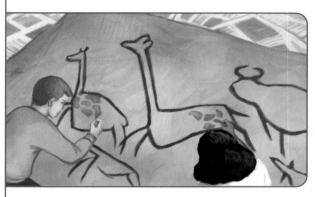

3 Add handprints by using charcoal to rub around your hands.

Review and Reflect

- What animals did you draw? What details did you include?
- How did you use lines, shapes, and colors to reflect the prehistoric style?
- What ideas or feelings does your mural express? How do you think your process compares to that of the cave artists?
- What prehistoric period does your mural represent? Explain.

Lesson 2

Ancient Mesopotamian Styles

The ancient Mesopotamians built some of the earliest cities. They invented one of the first writing systems. In math, they came up with the concepts of zero and place value. In architecture, they invented the arch. They are credited with the invention of the wheel by many scholars. This culture relied on the wheel to transport objects. Given these accomplishments, it is not surprising that the ancient Mesopotamians also developed original styles in art.

Artist unknown, Mesopotamian. *Earthenware Bowl,* 10th century B.C. Victoria and Albert Museum, London.

Artist unknown, Middle-Eastern. *Pictograph tablet from Jamdat Nasr, near Kish, Iraq,* ca. 3000 B.C. Clay. Ashmolean Museum, Oxford, England.

What kinds of geometric shapes can be identified in the pictographs?

From Art to Writing

People used pictures to communicate simple messages for thousands of years. Then the Sumerians in Mesopotamia invented a better system of writing. Their system began as **pictographs,** pictures that stand for words or objects. Over time, the pictures became simpler and gradually became symbols. The Sumerians created the symbols in soft clay tablets with a wedge-shaped reed. This type of writing is called **cuneiform.** The term comes from Latin and means "wedge form." Many of these clay tablets, such as the one shown above, tell about business details.

Research

Three important civilizations rose and fell in Mesopotamia. Do research to learn about the Sumerians, Babylonians, and Assyrians. In your Sketchbook Journal, make notes and draw examples about the art styles of each culture.

205

Cylinder *Impressions*

Artist unknown, Mesopotamian. *Cylinder Seal and Impression,* ca. 3300 B.C. Green jasper seal, height 1 inch. Musée du Louvre, Paris.

How many times was the design carved into the stone to make the impression shown?

Much of the artwork made by the people of ancient Mesopotamia was in the form of useful objects. Some of these included utensils for eating and drinking, baskets, board games, and toys. The cylinder seal above was carved from a piece of stone. It was sometimes used like a signature is used today. It made an impression that identified the person who owned the seal. Notice these details:

- Many cultures have made seals in the shape of a circle or square, like today's rubber stamps. The inventive Sumerians of southern Mesopotamia made theirs in the shape of a cylinder. It could be rolled onto soft clay to create a bas-relief design.
- The design was carved into the stone twice, creating a pattern when rolled onto the clay.

Mesopotamian Style

The animals shown are mythical beasts created from a combination of the artist's imagination and observation of real animals. They are also shown in profile. Where have you seen this style before?

Technique Tip

Carving Clay

When carving wet clay, clean the end of the carving tool often. Wipe it on a piece of newsprint or paper towel. After you clean the tool, dip the tip in water before your next impression. The tool will stick less in the clay and make it easier to create detailed designs.

Studio 2

Design a Cylinder Seal

Use what you have learned about Mesopotamian art to make a personal cylinder seal.

Materials

- ✓ newsprint
- ✓ pencil
- ✓ 3" × 4" piece of self-hardening clay
- ✓ clay tools
- ✓ modeling clay

1 Draw designs for a cylinder seal. Include animals and other personal objects.

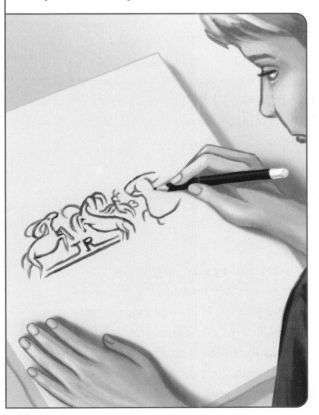

2 Roll a 3" × 4" piece of clay into a cylinder shape about three inches in diameter. Use clay tools to carve your design.

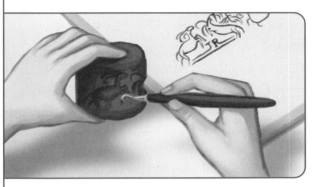

3 After the seal has dried, roll it over a slab of modeling clay to see the design.

Review and Reflect

- Describe the animals and objects in your design.
- In what ways are the animals real, and in what ways are they imaginary?
- What does the design say about you? How would you translate the design into words?
- Does your design make a good "signature"? Explain.

Lesson 3

Styles of Ancient Egypt

Many cultures have built large and impressive works of art. However, the ancient Egyptians exceeded all others in sheer size. Their rulers, called pharaohs, built giant pyramids. The pyramids became tombs for the pharaohs after death. The Great Pyramid of Khufu is the largest stone building in the world. It covers twelve acres and contains 2.5 million stone blocks that weigh about six thousand tons apiece. How such large stones could be transported to such heights and placed with such precision remains a mystery.

The rulers of ancient Egypt were entombed with artistic treasures of gold and jewels. The tomb walls were adorned with paintings showing the deceased in an afterlife. But ancient thieves robbed the great pyramids of the treasures. In an effort to prevent this, pharaohs later built their tombs below ground in the Valley of the Kings near ancient Thebes. Elaborate tombs were also created for ancient Egyptian queens in the Valley of the Queens. The most notable of these is the tomb of Queen Nefertari, who reigned with her husband, Ramesses II.

Architect unknown, Egyptian. *Pyramids of Khafre, Khufu, and Menkaure,* 2650–2575 B.C. Giza, Egypt.

The pyramids at Giza are the only one of the Seven Wonders of the Ancient World still standing.

Artist unknown, Egyptian. *Offering Bearers from the Tomb of Sebekhotep, Thebes,* ca. 1400 B.C. Tempera on mud plaster, 29 inches. The Metropolitan Museum of Art, New York.

How has the artist indicated space in this painting?

Egyptian Painting

The artists of ancient Egypt had an established set of rules called a **canon** that they followed as they created their works of art. The canon included a **module,** a unit of measurement used to draw the proportions of the human body. The Egyptians' canon led to a style of painting and drawing that is unique to this civilization. For example, notice that some people in the wall painting above are shown with their bodies facing forward, or in frontal view, but their legs and heads are in profile. This view is part of the canon and is one feature of ancient Egyptian style. The artist's use of overlapping gives the illusion of space.

Sketchbook Journal

The ancient Egyptians used a clenched fist as a unit of measurement for drawing human proportions. Use your clenched fist to measure yourself. For example, how many fists long are your arms and legs? Write down your measurements and use them to draw yourself in proportion.

Ancient *Egyptian Style*

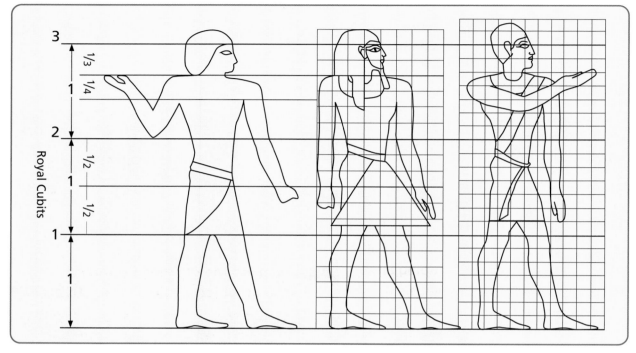

How is the human form in this diagram of the Egyptian canon divided into cubits?

This diagram shows the proportions used by the ancient Egyptians to draw people. In today's units of measure, a cubit equals about eighteen inches. Notice these details:

- Shoulders are much wider than hips. The waist is narrow and the body is slim.
- These proportions suggest health, well-being, and peace. Egyptian paintings often show people who are cheerful and calm.

Style and Perspective

Ancient Egyptian drawings and paintings almost always show people in action: working, playing music, or dancing. The most important figure appears larger than other figures. Women usually appear in light colors, and men in dark. Animal figures often represent the Egyptian gods. To show depth, distant objects appear smaller and near the top or bottom of the artwork.

Technique Tip

Using the Canon

The key to the Egyptian canon is to keep proportions the same. Look at the fractions on the left side of the diagram. They tell what fraction of a cubit each part of the head or body should be. No matter what unit of measure you use, the face should be one-third of the unit, from the knees to the feet should be one unit, and so on.

Studio 3

Draw in the Egyptian Style

Use what you have learned about ancient Egyptian style to draw yourself as an Egyptian.

Materials

- ✓ 12" × 18" white drawing paper
- ✓ pencil
- ✓ black marker
- ✓ colored pencils or markers

1 Use the Egyptian canon to make a full-length drawing of yourself doing an everyday activity, such as playing a sport or reading.

2 Add symbols to reflect the activity and your personality. Outline your drawing with a black marker.

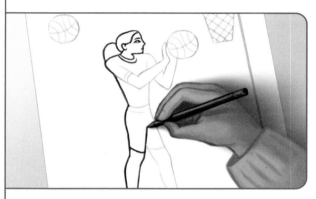

3 Complete the drawing by adding animals, objects, colors, and details.

Review and Reflect

- What activity did you show yourself performing? Why does this choice reflect the Egyptian style?
- How does your drawing reflect the Egyptian canon?
- How would you describe the meaning of your Egyptian-style drawing?
- What limits did using the canon impose on you?

The Styles of Ancient Greece

Do you recognize the buildings shown below and on page 213? The Parthenon was built in Greece nearly twenty-five hundred years ago. The Lincoln Memorial, on page 213, was completed in Washington, D.C. in 1922. These buildings show a link between two cultures. The ideas and styles of ancient Greece have shaped modern American architecture in many ways. What features do the two buildings have in common? What other influences have the ancient Greeks had on American culture?

amphora

hydria

krater

kylix

How do the shapes of these containers give clues to their uses?

Ictinus and Callicrates, architects. *Parthenon,* ca. 447–432 B.C. Athens, Greece.

The series of columns often used in Greek architecture allowed exterior and interior spaces to flow together.

Henry Bacon, architect. *Lincoln Memorial,* 1914–1922. Washington, D.C.

Ancient Greek Architecture

Ancient Greek architecture includes three orders: Doric, Ionic, and Corinthian. Each of these orders reflects a different column style. The Doric order is the earliest and was used for noble monuments, such as the Parthenon. This column style is still used today in homes and commercial buildings.

The Parthenon and the Lincoln Memorial both show features of the architectural style of ancient Greece. Each structure has Doric columns that form the front face, or **facade,** of the buildings. At the top of the Parthenon you will see what is left of the **pediment,** a triangular wall of stone on top of the facade. The pediment on the Lincoln Memorial is a low rectangle. This sets it apart from its ancient forerunner. Both buildings, though, have strong geometric shapes with little decoration.

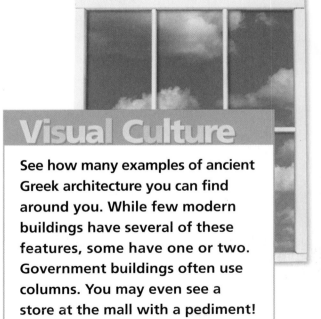

Visual Culture

See how many examples of ancient Greek architecture you can find around you. While few modern buildings have several of these features, some have one or two. Government buildings often use columns. You may even see a store at the mall with a pediment!

Attributed to Colmar Painter. *Interior of red-figured Kylix*, ca. 480. Terra cotta.

How is the style of these figures similar to those created by the Egyptians?

A common painting surface for ancient Greek artists was the clay of vases and other objects. The painting above appears on the inside of a **kylix,** a shallow drinking cup with two handles. Notice these details:

- The design is painted in what is called **red-figured style.** The artist left the figures on the red terra-cotta clay unpainted and colored the background black.
- The figures fill the circular space. Facial expressions and clothing are painted in great detail.

An Enduring Legacy

Paintings on Greek vessels show scenes from legends, gods and goddesses, or people in everyday life. The permanence of pottery makes these artworks valuable to both archaeologists and art collectors. The paintings provide a record of a society whose ideas are part of the foundation of our own.

Technique Tip

Using Ink

To make fine, controlled lines and detailed drawings in ink, choose a smooth surface that is not too absorbent. When filling spaces with ink, begin at the top of the artwork and work your way down. This will help prevent smearing the wet ink.

Studio 4

Create a Kylix Design

Use what you have learned about Greek painting to create a design for a kylix.

Materials

- ✓ 12" × 12" orange, gold, or rust-colored construction paper
- ✓ compass, pencil, and eraser
- ✓ India ink and paintbrush
- ✓ felt-tip pen (optional)
- ✓ scissors ⚠
- ✓ glue or glue stick
- ✓ heavy black paper

1 Use a compass to draw a circle to fill the paper. Draw a second circle one-half inch smaller than the first.

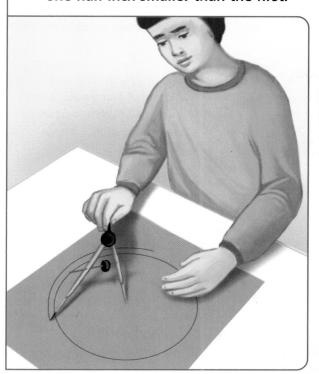

2 Draw a scene from Greek mythology or everyday life in the circle. Fill in the negative space with India ink and a paintbrush.

3 Add a border design using India ink or black felt-tip pen. Cut out your kylix design and mount it on black paper.

Review and Reflect

- What is the subject of your kylix design?
- How do the lines and shapes you included reflect the Greek style?
- What does your design say about the subject?
- If you were to create an actual kylix from clay, would you paint it with this design? Explain.

Lesson 5

The Roman Style

The Romans built the largest and most powerful empire in ancient history. They used their art styles and building techniques to construct roads and bridges. Many of these structures still stand. **Aqueducts,** like the one shown below, carried water to cities. Although the Sumerians invented the arch, the Romans put it to use in construction throughout their vast empire. Today the arch is regarded as a major feature of Roman architecture.

Architect unknown, Roman. *Pont du Gard,* 20–10 B.C. Approximately 150 by 900 feet. Nîmes, France.

The layers of the aqueduct served as both a bridge (first level) and a water system (top level). Such a structure was not possible without the arch.

Based on this portrait sculpture, what kind of emperor do you think Caracalla was?

Roman Busts

Architecture was not the only art form that helped Romans rule their empire. Portraits of the emperor appeared everywhere to remind conquered people that they were under his rule. **Busts** are portrait sculptures that show the head and neck, and sometimes shoulders, of a person. Notice the realistic details in this bust of Emperor Antoninus. He was nicknamed Caracalla, the word for the cloak he wore. He was considered a cruel, violent man. This bust reminded people of his power. How is his strong personality reflected in this bust?

Research

Do research to learn more about Roman architecture and sculpture. Find out what building material the Romans invented that is still popular today. Also explore other Roman art forms, such as mosaic. Look for these elements of Roman style in your environment.

Artist unknown, Roman. *Coin with a Portrait of Constantine,* 27 B.C.–A.D. 396. Bronze. Castello Sforzesca, Milan, Italy.

Which two views did the artist use to show the figure?

The Roman Empire also used coins as a constant reminder of the emperor's power. The emperors produced a common currency for use throughout the empire. The coins helped to unify the empire and to encourage trade. Many coins bore a portrait of the emperor and reminded distant subjects that they were under Roman rule. Some coins, such as this one, were decorated with the emperor's image on one side and another image on the opposite side. This side of the coin shows a female figure representing the goddess Fortuna, the Roman goddess of fate and good fortune. Notice these details:

- The goddess is shown holding a cornucopia, symbolizing fortune and prosperity.
- From the waist up, the figure is shown in frontal view. From the waist down, she is shown in three-quarter view.
- As in the Greek kylikes, the woman and her dress are shown in detail.

Greek Influences

Roman art was strongly influenced by the Greek style that came before it. The Greeks were among the first to mint coins and the first to put rulers' portraits on them. The Romans also learned about sculpture from the Greeks, who showed idealized human figures in their sculptures. However, Roman busts were more realistic and showed people as they actually appeared.

Technique Tip

Reversed Lettering

Make a pattern of words in reverse by first writing the letters on several layers of paper. Press hard as you write. Flip the top paper over and write over the indentations made by your pencil. Use this reversed pattern to transfer the letters to your coin.

Studio 5

Create an Embossed Coin Design

Commemorate a person or event by making a Roman-style coin design.

Materials

- ✓ 12" diameter cardboard circle
- ✓ 14" × 14" sheet of aluminum or copper foil
- ✓ pad of newspaper or newsprint
- ✓ embossing tools, such as craft sticks and cotton swabs
- ✓ glue
- ✓ India ink or black shoe polish
- ✓ steel wool or soft cloth

1 Make sketches for your coin design. Place the foil face down on a pad of papers. Transfer your design to the foil with pencil. Remember to work in reverse.

2 Use embossing tools to carefully create a raised design. Glue the foil to the cardboard circle, folding the edges over.

3 Apply India ink or black shoe polish over the entire surface. Let dry. Gently rub the surface with steel wool or a soft cloth.

Review and Reflect

- Describe your commemorative coin. What details did you show?
- What techniques of your coin design do you think Romans might have used?
- What does your coin design convey about the person or event it commemorates?
- On what type of coin would you like to see your design minted? Explain.

Meet *the Artist*

Mesopotamian Artists

Mesopotamia is a region between the Tigris and Euphrates Rivers. Many different civilizations rose and fell there. Mesopotamia still exists and is now known as central Iraq. The ancient people and the great cities they built are gone. However, modern civilization would be very different if it were not for the achievements of ancient Mesopotamian cultures.

Artist unknown, Mesopotamian. *Gudea, King of Lagash,* 2120 B.C. Diorite. Musée du Louvre, Paris.

King Gudea had extensive temples built during his reign over Lagash, now called Telloh in present-day southeastern Iraq.

"But upon you he will shower down abundance, The choicest birds, the rarest fishes. The land shall have its fill of harvest riches. He who at dusk orders the hush-greens, Will shower down upon you a rain of wheat." —THE EPIC OF GILGAMESH

Rolling Forward

The Sumerians were the first people to build cities in Mesopotamia. Their food crops were grown in irrigated fields. A plentiful food supply gave them a chance to develop other skills.

Sumerians became expert at building and working with metal. They developed trade with other cultures and created a writing system to record the trade. They also discovered the use of wheels, which made moving goods from place to place an easier task. These creations gave the Sumerians wealth and power.

A King, an Epic, and an Empire

Each Sumerian city was ruled by a king. One of these kings, Gilgamesh, is the hero of a group of stories. *The Epic of Gilgamesh* is one of the most important and perhaps oldest written stories.

Sumerians built giant temples called ziggurats. They are similar to pyramids, except their sides are stepped, not angled.

King Sargon built a powerful Sumerian empire and at one time he ruled all of Mesopotamia. But Sumeria was overrun by invaders in about 2000 B.C. Later, two civilizations, Babylon and Assyria, arose in ancient Mesopotamia.

Talk About It

- Do you think ancient Mesopotamia was a good place to be an artist? Explain.

- How many years passed between the beginning and the end of Sumerian civilization?

Ancient Mesopotamia

5500 B.C.

ca. **5000** B.C.
Sumerians develop world's first cities; use copper

4500 B.C.

Sumerian writing tablet

Sumerians invent world's first writing
ca. **3500** B.C. — 3500 B.C.

Sumerians work with bronze
ca. **3100** B.C.

ca. **3000** B.C.
Sumerians invent the wheel

King Gilgamesh

ca. **2700** B.C.
King Gilgamesh rules Uruk

Ziggurat at Ur

ca. **2500** B.C. — 2500 B.C.
Ziggurat of King Urnammu built at Ur

ca. **2300** B.C.
Sargon the Great rules Sumeria

ca. **2000** B.C.
Sumerian civilization overrun by invaders

1500 B.C.

Look *and Compare*

Ancient Sculptures in Two Styles

Sculpture was a popular art form in ancient cultures. Usually, artworks showed rulers or gods and goddesses. Yet the materials, techniques, and styles differed from one group to another. And as you have read, the time periods of ancient cultures and their artworks covers a large span of time. The sculptures shown on page 223 were made more than two thousand years apart.

Some modern sculptors still use traditional materials and ancient techniques.

A Mesopotamian Sculpture

Stone was scarce in Mesopotamia. Buildings were made with bricks of hardened mud. What little stone could be found was used for important artworks such as *Statue of an Orant*. It shows the calf-length skirt that both men and women wore at the time. In other ways, though, this sculpture is not realistic at all. Notice the exaggerated proportion of the arms in relation to the figure. The eyes and pupils are also exaggerated. In many sculptures, the eyes were further emphasized by inlaying colored materials. By altering the proportions of the eyes, the artist made them the focal point of this sculpture.

A Roman Sculpture

The *Statue of Togato Barberini* was made about twenty-five hundred years later than the sculpture above it. The Romans had been influenced by the Greek idea that all persons had value. Therefore, the subject of this sculpture was neither a ruler nor a god, although he was a leading citizen. He is holding busts of his forebears—probably his father and grandfather. All three faces are highly realistic, with good reason. Romans of the time made wax impressions of people at their death. These were sometimes used to help create a sculpture in marble, as in these two busts.

Artist unknown, Mesopotamian.
Statue of an Orant, ca. 2400 B.C.

Artist unknown, Roman. *Statue of Togato Barberini*, A.D. 1st century.

Compare & Contrast

- In what ways are these two sculptures alike?

- What does each sculpture tell you about the time and culture in which it was made?

223

The Medieval Style

The Medieval period, or **Middle Ages,** lasted from the fall of Rome in A.D. 410 to about 1450. It was the time of castles and knights, battles and plagues. It was also a time when religion played an important role in people's lives and in art. Some of the largest-scale artworks of the time are the cathedrals that still stand throughout Europe. The cathedral at Chartres, shown here, is one of the most well-known.

What similarities do this sand castle and *Chartres Cathedral* share?

Various architects. *Chartres Cathedral, West Façade,* ca. A.D. 1028–1215.

What types of balance do you notice in this cathedral?

Artist unknown. (Detail) *Bayeux Tapestry: The English Landing in Normandy,* A.D. 11th century. Wool on linen, 20 by 231 feet. Musée de la Tapisserie, Bayeux, France.

Compare this tapestry to the *Standard of Ur* on page 198. What similarities do you see?

Medieval Tapestries

Tapestries were another favorite art form of medieval times. Artists wove or stitched detailed pictures in each tapestry to tell a visual story. The artwork above shows a small section of the *Bayeux Tapestry.*

The tapestry was traditionally attributed to Queen Matilda, wife of William I. It was believed to have been made by the women of her court. The French even called it "Queen Matilda's Tapestry." Others contend that the artwork was commissioned by William's half brother, Bishop Odo of Bayeux.

The entire artwork is about 231 feet long and its pictures tell about an important time in English history. When King Edward died, William of Normandy invaded England with his army and won the Battle of Hastings in 1066. What part of this story is told in the detail shown above?

Sketchbook Journal

Make a sketch of a medieval castle. You may rely on your own ideas and what you already know about castles, or, if you like, do some research to learn about real castles of the Middle Ages. Draw your castle in an interesting setting, such as high on a hill or deep in a forest.

Castle *Architecture*

James of St. George. *Beaumaris Castle,* ca. 1294. Anglesley, North Wales.

What types of forms did the architect use?

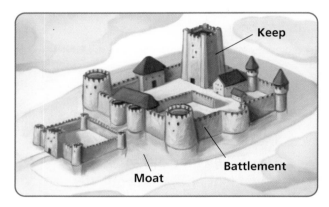

Identify the main parts of a castle and note their placement and relationship to one another.

When you think of castles, you might think of exciting tales of brave knights and beautiful princesses. When medieval architects thought of castles, they thought only of brutal invaders. Notice these details about *Beaumaris Castle* in Wales:

- The only openings are narrow slits through which defenders could shoot arrows.

- The overall design is a series of mostly geometric forms.
- The castle once had a moat that was eighteen feet wide. Over time, parts of the moat have been filled in.

Parts of a Castle

The moat was only one of many elements designed to make a castle safe from attack. Defenders could hide behind the battlements and fire arrows down at attackers. Most castles were surrounded by at least one wall. Beaumaris Castle was surrounded by four walls, one inside the other! Castles really did have dungeons, sometimes located in the keep, the main stronghold of the castle. All these features helped to keep the castle's lord and lady, family members, and serfs safe.

Technique Tip

Slab Method

When using the slab method to work with clay, use a rolling pin to roll the clay about one-half inch thick. To join two slabs, score the edges of both slabs with a toothpick or toothbrush. Apply slip, a soupy mixture of clay and water, to both scored edges, and press and smooth the edges together.

Studio 6

Create a Model of a Castle Keep

Use what you have learned about castles to make a clay model of a keep.

Materials

- ✓ castle sketches from Sketchbook Journal
- ✓ ceramic clay
- ✓ 14" square of heavy cardboard
- ✓ clay tools
- ✓ containers for water
- ✓ cotton rags
- ✓ plastic bags
- ✓ newsprint
- ✓ rolling pins or cardboard cylinders

1 Use your sketch ideas to plan a castle keep. Roll slabs of clay one-half inch thick. Cut and connect the slabs to form the walls of the keep. Use the cardboard as the base.

2 Once your square or cylinder is complete, add windows, arches, battlements, and other details. Cover with damp rags and plastic. Allow to dry to a leather hard stage.

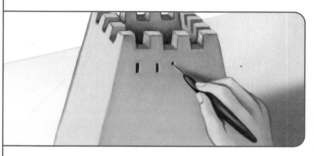

3 Use clay tools to incise grooves and lines in the clay to mimic stone. Allow your model to dry slowly and completely.

Review and Reflect

- Describe the shapes and details you included in your castle keep model.
- How did you use line, shape, and texture to show the parts of your castle model?
- What mood do you think your castle would convey to a visitor or an invader?
- In what country and setting do you envision your model being built? Explain.

The Renaissance

The word *renaissance* means "rebirth." The period called the **Renaissance** brought a rebirth of the styles of ancient Greece and Rome following the Middle Ages. Recall what you read about the realistic busts of Roman emperors. Renaissance artists also made realistic portraits of everyday people, as well as images of nature. New ways of thinking and seeing arose in the Renaissance. Notice the realistic qualities of the painting below compared to those in previous lessons in this unit.

Albrecht Altdorfer. *Landscape with Footbridge,* ca. 1518–1520. Oil on vellum on wood, 16 3/8 by 13 7/8 inches. National Gallery, London.

Piero della Francesca. (Detail)
Scene from Legend of the True Cross, 1456–1466. Fresco, 131 by 291 inches. Church of San Francesco, Arezzo, Italy.

Renaissance Portraits

Scene from Legend of the True Cross shows part of a series of paintings by Italian artist Piero della Francesca (ca. 1420–1492). This scene is an example of Renaissance style, showing the subjects painted in realistic detail. The composition is balanced and the foreground colors are clear and bright. The background has a dark, hazy quality that is common in paintings of the time. Piero della Francesca was not only an artist but also a mathematician. The Renaissance brought a new focus on art, science, and learning. Many people, such as Leonardo da Vinci, were skilled in more than one area.

Sketchbook Journal

Renaissance artists had a new interest in showing people and nature in lifelike detail. Gather and make sketches of two or three different fruits. Then cut the fruits open and draw these cross-section views. Show details such as seeds, peels, sections, and variations in color and texture.

Leonardo da Vinci. *Madonna of the Rocks,* 1483–1485. Oil on panel, 78 by 48 inches. Musée du Louvre, Paris.

How does this painting show Leonardo's interest in nature?

Leonardo da Vinci, whom you read about in Unit 1, was one of the most well-known Renaissance artists. *Madonna of the Rocks* shows his use of aerial perspective, also called atmospheric perspective. Notice the techniques that Leonardo used to show depth and distance:

- The foreground is lighter than the background. Colors are brighter and more distinct.
- Figures and objects in the foreground are shown in more detail than objects in the background.

An Eye for Nature

Leonardo is best known for his portraits. He valued the beauty of nature as well. As this painting shows, he saw people as being at home in nature. Notice how the rocks seem to shelter the people. Leonardo also included water and sunlight. He used contrast to show the light source, which appears to shine from the left side of the painting. What effect does this have in the painting?

Technique Tip

Ink Techniques
When drawing with pen and ink, you can use various techniques to create a range of values and effects. Experiment with drawing on damp paper to create soft, feathery lines. Dilute ink and apply with a brush to fill in light areas. After the ink is dry, you can use white ink or oil pastel to add highlights.

Studio 7

Draw a Rocky Landscape

Use what you have learned about Renaissance art to draw a rocky landscape.

Materials

- ✓ 12" × 18" white drawing paper
- ✓ pencil
- ✓ pen and India ink
- ✓ rocks

1 Collect some rocks of various sizes, shapes, and textures. Arrange them into a miniature landscape.

2 Use a pencil to draw the landscape on white drawing paper. Then complete the drawing with pen and India ink.

3 Use your imagination to add trees, plants, and other natural elements. Plan a balanced composition.

Review and Reflect

- How would you describe the place you have represented in your landscape?
- How did you show distance in your drawing?
- What does your drawing convey about nature?
- What would you do next time to improve your landscape?

The Art of Native America

The Apache, Cherokee, Hopi, Iroquois, Navajo, and Sioux are some of the Native American cultures, or nations. They also refer to ways of life. The many native peoples of North America have their own languages, customs, and art forms. Yet these cultures are linked by at least one common bond: their bond with nature. Nature provides the materials, the subjects, and the inspiration for Native American art.

Artist unknown, Assiniboine culture. *Warrior's Shirt,* ca. 1870–1900. Animal hide with beads. Photo © Christie's Images/Corbis.

When the arms are held out from the body during a ceremonial dance, the decorative patterns and fringed leather of the shirt resemble wings.

Artist unknown, Hopi. *Kachina Doll with Horns and Feathers.* The Heard Museum, Phoenix, AZ.

What parts of the kachina suggest the Earth spirit that inspired it?

Hopi Kachinas

For hundreds of years, the Hopi people farmed the deserts of the Southwest. Their main crop was corn, but they also grew beans and squashes. They later incorporated crops from Europe, Asia, and Africa, such as watermelons and other fruits.

Their reliance on their crops made it necessary for them to remain in one location. This allowed them more time to develop their artistic skills of weaving and pottery making. The Hopi were also skilled at making baskets and other textile arts.

They lived in pueblos, or self-ruled villages. Their houses were made from packed earth and fiber, perhaps like those of the earlier Anasazi who are thought to be their ancestors.

This doll, made for a Hopi child, represents a kachina, or spirit being. In the Hopi culture, kachinas are helpful messengers. Their main role is to bring precious rain to the desert. These dolls are given to children to help them learn the names and likenesses of actual kachinas. The dolls are carved from cottonwood roots, painted, and clothed.

The Hopi call their ancestors "People of Long Ago." Today, many Hopi continue to practice their cultural traditions, including farming and artistic crafts.

Research

Do research to learn about some symbols and images that are important to Native American peoples. Draw your favorite symbols and images in your Sketchbook Journal. Make notes about what culture each one is from and what meanings it has.

Art *of the* Apache

Like the Hopi, the Apache also live in the Southwest. Some Apache eventually settled and took up farming. Most relied on hunting and gathering until modern times. Notice these details in this Apache basket:

- The symbols and images are clearly those of a people who are hunters rather than farmers.
- The use of geometric shapes stands out against the overall organic shape of the basket. Note the symmetry.

The Art of Basketmaking

Different Native American groups used different methods to make baskets. The basket on this page was made of a grass-like fiber using the **coiling** method. Starting from the bottom, each coil is placed on top of the previous coil and stitched in place. Other groups used the **twining** method in which two or more warp fibers are woven between vertical weft fibers. Some used the **plaiting** method in which the warp and weft fibers are woven at right angles to one another. Both are a form of weaving, differing in the angles at which the fibers cross. Native Americans used materials such as wool, feathers, and plant fibers to weave their basket designs.

Artist unknown, Western Apache. *Basket*, 19th century. Willow and fiber, 21 ¼ by 7 ½ inches. Nelson-Atkins Museum of Art, Kansas City, MO. Purchase: Nelson Trust, 33–1312. Photo by Tim Thayer.

What geometric shapes are used in the design of this basket?

Technique Tip

Coil Technique

When making a coil basket, artists use many separate pieces of fiber or other materials. As you begin and end a color of yarn, wrap the first few inches of each new piece under the last few inches of the piece you are finishing. This method makes the coil wraps appear seamless.

Make a Coil Basket

Use what you have learned about Native American art to make a coil basket.

Materials

- ✓ 5' length of ³/₁₆" cotton clothesline
- ✓ 4-ply yarn in a variety of colors
- ✓ large plastic tapestry needle ⓢ
- ✓ scissors ⓢ

1 Prepare the coils by wrapping the clothesline with yarn. Thread a length of yarn onto the needle. Hold the end in place as you wrap slip knots over it to start.

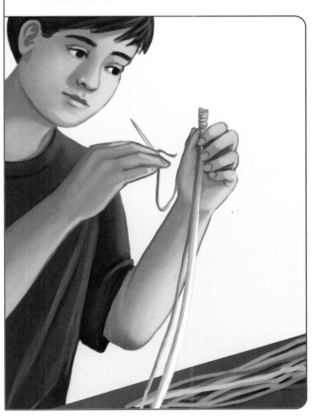

2 Wrap the length of clothesline with yarn. Every three wraps, draw your needle through a loop to make a slip knot. This will keep your wraps in place.

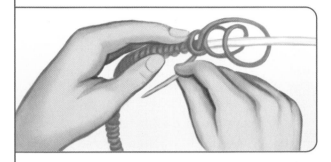

3 Spiral the coil to begin the basket. Stitch each coil to the previous one. Coil to the outside edge to widen the opening. Coil to the inside edge to narrow it.

Review and Reflect

- Describe the form of your coil basket and the fibers you used.
- How did you use colors, textures, and shapes to create a design or pattern?
- How do the lines and form of your basket affect its function and purpose?
- What would you do differently the next time you made a coil basket?

Eastern Art Styles

Eastern art includes artworks from China and Japan in the Far East, India in South Asia, parts of the Middle East, and many other Asian nations. Asian cultures grew separately from European cultures for thousands of years. The building shown below is an example of Eastern architecture.

Mughal emperor Shah Jehan was so devastated by the death of his wife, Mumtaz Mahal, that he had this mausoleum built to honor her. It took the more than twenty thousand workers twenty-two years to complete. The building's elaborate design and details include precious stones inlaid in floral and intertwining geometric designs. The building's name is a shortened version of Mumtaz Mahal, which means "Chosen One of the Palace."

Ustad Ahmad, architect. *Taj Mahal,* 1653. Agra, India.

Where is the dome's form repeated in the design?

Yüan Chiang. *Carts on a Winding Mountain Road,* 1694. Hanging scroll, ink and color on silk, 71 1/4 by 36 3/4 inches. Nelson-Atkins Museum of Art, Kansas City, MO. Purchase: Nelson Trust, 35-151.

Nature and religion play an important part in Eastern art. The subjects of scrolls often include flowers, birds, landscapes, and temple icons. Paths or roads help lead the viewer into the landscape paintings. Majestic mountains help draw the viewer's eye from top to bottom. The artists' use of perspective sometimes includes more than one vanishing point. What effect might this have on landscape paintings?

This landscape by Chinese artist Yüan Chiang (1694–1725) shows one style that was popular in eastern Asia. Notice that the artist used organic lines to show the landscape and geometric lines to show buildings and the bridge. Observe the size relationships of the people, the buildings, and the mountain. What do you think the artist is saying about people and nature?

Compare this landscape to some examples from Western art. Look for similarities and differences in style.

Sketchbook Journal

Observe or collect fabrics and wallpapers that are printed with scenes from nature. Are the natural elements shown in realistic detail, or are they simplified? Draw several designs using objects from nature. Note which design you think would make a pleasing fabric or wallpaper design.

Scroll Painting

The Eastern art of scroll painting dates back to the fourth century A.D. Early scrolls included the illustrated scrolls of China and the narrative scrolls of Japan, and were created with inks on silk or paper.

Artist unknown, Japanese. *Kimono*, 20th century. Silk with embroidery. Seattle Art Museum, Seattle, WA.

How is the artist's design on this kimono similar to the Chinese scroll painting on page 237?

Textile arts, such as the kimono shown here, have been produced in Japan for centuries. The kimono originated in China, but came to represent a form of social status in Japan. Kimonos are still worn today by women and men for special occasions or ceremonies. Many Japanese artists today continue the textile traditions of their ancestors. As you study this kimono, look for these details:

- The embroidered design shows objects from nature. The cascading flower design leads the viewer's eye to the birds, flowers, and water below.
- The bold, swirling lines of the water are less realistic and add interest.

Silk, Canvas of the East

Both the Chinese and the Japanese artworks were created on silk. The Chinese were the first to develop the craft of silkmaking. They kept it secret for centuries. Because silk was soft, strong, and beautiful, Europeans paid high prices for it when they began trading with China. In fact, the first trade routes between Europe and China were called the Silk Road.

Technique Tip

Patterns
To create interesting patterns, try repeating some elements and varying others. For example, repeat the same shapes in different colors or sizes. Or, repeat the same design but reverse the colors of the objects and the background. Remember, a design does not have to be made up of geometric shapes. A design may not need shapes at all.

Studio 9

Design a Japanese Robe

Use what you have learned about Eastern art to draw a design for a silk robe.

Materials

- ✓ large sheet of white construction paper
- ✓ pencil
- ✓ newsprint
- ✓ markers and pens, including pens with metallic inks

1 Draw the outline of a Japanese-style robe on construction paper. On newsprint, draw some designs for the robe.

2 Use a pencil to draw the final design on the construction paper outline. Color the design with markers and pens.

3 Use pens with metallic inks to add silver and/or gold accents to your design.

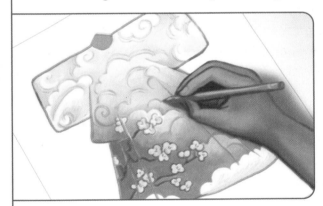

Review and Reflect

- How would you describe the design of your robe to a person who could not see it?
- What features of the design make it Eastern in style?
- Why did you choose the pattern you did?
- If you were to design another robe, what would you try next?

Lesson 10

Modern Art Styles

The **Industrial Revolution,** or "machine age," had its influences on art. Products were mass-produced, cities grew, and economies began to prosper. With its beginnings in England, the revolution soon spread across Europe and North America.

Artists were no longer under the service of the church or political powers. With the invention of photography, they no longer had to capture their subjects in a realistic style. As a result, new art movements emerged. Artists began using the changing social and economic times as subjects for art.

The painting below by French artist Berthe Morisot (1841–1895) is an example of the freedom of the modern style. Although the painting is not realistic, the viewer can recognize the subject. Morisot's bold brushstrokes and use of color reflect her impression of the scene.

Berthe Morisot. *Summer's Day,* 1879. Oil on canvas, 18 by 29 ¼ inches. National Gallery, London.

How is this painting an example of a modern style?

Joseph Mallord William Turner. *Rain, Steam, and Speed: The Great Western Railway,* 1844. Oil on canvas, 35 by 47 ⅝ inches. The National Gallery, London.

How does Turner's style convey the train's speed?

Impressionism

Artists' newfound freedom of expression led Berthe Morisot, Claude Monet, Camille Pissarro, and other French artists to develop a new art movement. **Impressionism** showed the effects of light and color on everyday subjects. Impressionist artists wanted viewers to see the relationships between colors, patterns, and textures. Their artworks omitted realistic details. How do Morisot's painting on page 240, and Turner's painting on this page, reflect the Impressionist style?

Artists' cultural heritage also influenced modern art styles. American artist Lois Mailou Jones (1905–1998) painted her impression of African masks in *Les Fétiches.* She used bold colors, lines, and shapes to express her heritage. Notice how her use of light and brushstrokes resembles the style of the Impressionists. What other similarities do you notice in these artworks?

Lois Mailou Jones. *Les Fétiches (The Fetishes),* 1938. Oil on canvas, 25 ½ by 21 ¼ inches. Smithsonian American Art Museum, Washington, D.C.

What culture and objects do you think inspired this painting?

Sketchbook Journal

Use colored markers to make Impressionist sketches of landscapes near your school or neighborhood. Try to capture the main objects and colors in each scene. Make sketches of the same landscape at different times of day to study the effect of light on a subject.

Max Beckmann. *Self-Portrait,* 1937. Oil on canvas, 75 by 34 inches. The Art Institute of Chicago, Chicago, IL.

How has emphasis been placed on the figure?

In the early twentieth century, a group of German artists considered the Impressionist style to be too naturalistic. They wanted their artworks to reflect a freer form of expression. From this desire, the Expressionist style emerged. **Expressionist** artists use distortion, exaggeration, bright colors, and bold lines to show their subjects. This self-

portrait by Max Beckmann (1884–1950) is an example of the Expressionist style. Look for these details as you study the artwork:

- The artist used simple shapes and strong colors.
- Beckmann exaggerated the proportions of facial features and hands.

Compare and Contrast

Think about how Impressionism and Expressionism are alike and different. Both styles show the main shapes and forms of a subject. Neither shows realistic details. Impressionists often used soft, muted colors. Expressionists usually used bright colors. Impressionists seldom painted bold solid lines. Instead, they used implied lines and shading techniques for figures and objects. Expressionists, though, often used actual lines like those in Beckmann's painting.

Technique Tip

Painting Clear, Bright Colors

Painting in the Expressionist style calls for clear, bright colors. To achieve them, make sure to rinse your brush in clean water each time you change colors. Blot it dry on a paper towel. To keep colors from running together, let an area dry before painting another color that touches it.

Studio 10

Paint an Expressionist Portrait

Use what you have learned about Expressionism to paint a portrait in this style.

Materials

- ✓ newsprint
- ✓ pencil
- ✓ 12" × 18" painting paper
- ✓ tempera or acrylic paints
- ✓ paintbrush

1 Use a pencil to draw the face of a classmate on newsprint.

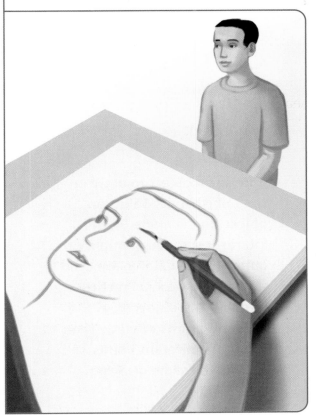

2 Decide what mood you want the portrait to express. Experiment with changing shapes and proportions to express the mood.

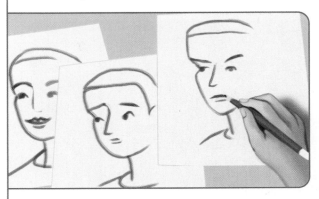

3 Transfer the final sketch to painting paper. Use appropriate lines and colors to complete an Expressionist portrait.

Review and Reflect

- How would you describe the person in your portrait?
- How did you use line and color to show the Expressionist style?
- What would be a good title for this portrait?
- What do you like best about the portrait?

Portfolio *Project*

Create a Cubist Self-Portrait

Juan Gris. *Portrait of Pablo Picasso,* 1912. Oil on canvas, 36 ⅝ by 29 ³/₁₆ inches. The Art Institute of Chicago, Chicago, IL.

Plan

The portrait above by Spanish artist Juan Gris (1887–1927) is an example of the Cubist style. In **Cubism** a subject is broken into parts and then "reassembled" into flat, abstracted shapes. Pablo Picasso and Georges Braque developed the Cubist style in the early twentieth century. It rejected the techniques of perspective and the idea that art should imitate nature.

Notice how Gris used angular shapes to show his form in two dimensions.

- The face is painted to show more than one view at once. What do you think Gris wanted to express through this unusual point of view?
- How does the Cubist style differ from Expressionism? Notice how the shapes in the two art styles differ.
- What could you express by using the Cubist style in a portrait?

Using what you have learned about this style, create your own Cubist portrait.

Sketchbook Journal

Choose an object to draw in the Cubist style. Select an object that is made up of interesting shapes. Simplify the object to draw it in geometric shapes and forms. Practice drawing the object from different points of view. Then show the different points of view in the same drawing.

Materials

- ✓ newsprint
- ✓ pencil
- ✓ mirror
- ✓ 12" × 18" white painting paper
- ✓ tempera paints
- ✓ paintbrush

Create

1 Look straight into a mirror to draw your face on newsprint. Then draw a side view from the left and another view from the right.

2 On painting paper, lightly draw your full-face view. Add your features as seen in the left and right side views, showing all three views in one sketch.

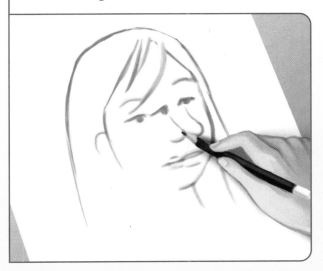

3 Simplify your face and features to show them as geometric shapes. Fill the background with geometric shapes. Use shapes to help express a mood.

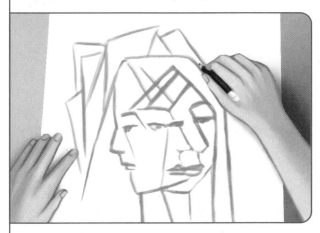

4 Paint your portrait with tempera. Choose a color scheme that expresses the mood you have chosen. Use varying values to add contrast to shapes.

Reflect

- What problems did you have while completing your self-portrait? How did you solve them?
- How did you use Cubist style to express a mood?
- What did you learn about the techniques you used?
- Talk to a classmate about the project. How are your self-portraits the same? How are they different?

Unit 5 *Review*

Vocabulary Review

A Match each art term below with its definition.

cuneiform	Cubism
aqueduct	Impressionism
Medieval period	Neolithic
Paleolithic	Renaissance
module	kylix

1. Middle Ages
2. New Stone Age
3. wedge-shaped
4. a style using flat, abstracted shapes
5. channel for water
6. emphasizing light, color, and emotion
7. drinking cup
8. rebirth
9. Old Stone Age
10. unit of measurement

Artists and Their Art

B Match each artwork in the box with the style below.

> *Cylinder Seal and Impression*
> *Madonna of the Rocks*
> *Beaker with Ibex Design*
> *Kachina Doll with Horns and Feathers*
> *Self-Portrait*
> *Pont du Gard*
> *Lincoln Memorial*
> *Bayeux Tapestry*
> *Carts on a Winding Mountain Road*
> *Pyramids of Khafre, Khufu, and Menkaure*

1. Egyptian
2. Greek
3. Native American
4. Expressionism
5. Mesopotamian
6. Medieval
7. Renaissance
8. Eastern
9. Roman
10. Prehistoric

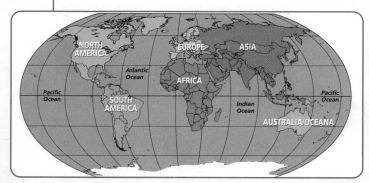

Artists and cultures worldwide have contributed to the history of art.

Respond to Art

C Look at *Haida Headdress Frontlet with Ancestor Figure.* Match each art term below with the letter in the illustration.

Attributed to Albert Edward Edenshaw. *Haida Headdress Frontlet with Ancestor Figure,* ca. 1870. Seattle Art Museum, Seattle, WA.

Art Terms

1. symmetrical balance
2. pattern
3. exaggerated proportion
4. complementary colors

Unit 5 *Review*

Write About Art

Write to Inform

D Look back at the artworks in this unit. Choose one from a culture that you find especially interesting. Do research to learn more about the time and place of the artwork's creation. If the artist is known, learn about the artist as well. Make a chart like the one below to guide your research. Then write an article about the artwork's historical background.

Name of Culture

What was life like for the artist who made the artwork?

_____

Was the society reflected in its art forms?

_____

How does the artwork reflect the time and place in which it was made?

_____

How did this chapter in art history influence today's artworks?

_____

Your Studio Work

E Answer these questions in your Sketchbook Journal or on a separate sheet of paper.

1. What style in this unit interested you the most? Explain what you found interesting about it.
2. What problems did you have as you experimented with each style? How did you solve them? What will you do differently next time?
3. Which artworks inspired your own art-making process? Which styles would you like to practice more?
4. Choose one artwork to keep in your portfolio. Tell why you chose it.

Put It All Together

Auguste Rodin. *Monument to Balzac,* 1897–1898. Bronze, 108 ³/₄ by 48 ¹/₄ by 41 inches. Museum of Modern Art, New York.

F **Discuss or write about Rodin's artwork using the four steps for critically viewing artwork.**

1. **Describe** How would you describe the style of this artwork? What adjectives describe the subject of the sculpture?
2. **Analyze** What cultures might have influenced the style of the sculpture? What clues help you figure this out?
3. **Interpret** What do you think Rodin wanted to express in this artwork? What qualities of the subject did the artist show? How do you think Rodin felt about Balzac?
4. **Judge** French artist Auguste Rodin (1840–1917) became known for his sculptures. Do you think this artwork demonstrates why this was so? Explain.

"Sculpture is an art of hollows and projections."
—AUGUSTE RODIN

Sculptor Auguste Rodin learned about art by visiting museums. He also traveled to Italy to see the artworks of Renaissance sculptor Michelangelo.

Maya Lin. *The Wave Field,* 1993. Earth sculpture, François-Xavier Bagnoud Building, University of Michigan, Ann Arbor, MI.

Unit 6

Careers in Art

What career might you choose in the field of visual arts? Would you paint large canvases in a studio? Would you create furniture for homes or schools? Or perhaps you would like to plan the gardens for a theme park.

Artists in the field of **fine arts** produce artworks such as paintings and sculptures to be viewed and appreciated. Many artists work in **applied arts,** creating artworks which are used from sofas to toasters. Artists in **design** careers plan how objects or places should look or be constructed. Design artists include interior designers and landscape architects. Other artists use skilled hands to produce **crafts,** such as quilts or metalworks.

Maya Lin chose to become an architect and a sculptor. She used her knowledge of both careers to design *The Wave Field.* As you discover the careers in this unit, consider how your knowledge of art might lead to a career in the world of visual art.

About *the Artist*

Maya Lin also designed the *Vietnam Veterans Memorial.* She was still in college when she won a nationwide contest for the memorial's design. Discover more about Lin's life and career on pages 268–269.

Illustrator

Many books you have read contain pictures and drawings. These **illustrations** help readers and viewers visually understand the text. Some **illustrators** create artworks for magazine and newspaper articles. Some illustrate books and product ads. These artists may rely on one or two favorite media. Others may experiment with many media and methods to convey a message.

Elizabeth Shippen Green. *Haunted at Moonlight with Bat, Owl and Ghostly Moth,* 1902. Charcoal drawing on illustration board. *Harper's Magazine.*

Illustrators work with a variety of media, techniques, and tools. Above, an artist uses a narrow brush and ink to add finishing touches to an illustration.

Arthur Rackham. *There is Almost Nothing that has Such a Keen Sense of Fun as a Fallen Leaf,* 1906. Stapleton Collection.

Kinds of Illustrators

Some illustrators use their talents for specific purposes. They create illustrations for fiction novels, textbooks, advertisements, or technical manuals. Some specialize in one subject, such as cars or outer space.

Illustrators like Arthur Rackham use imagination and media to bring an author's words to life. They may create these visuals using only pen and ink. Or they might add a splash of color with a watercolor wash. Other illustrators use **digital technology,** such as computers, graphics tablets, and scanners to help tell a visual story.

For what purpose was the illustration above created? How did Rackham show that a gusty wind is blowing?

Sketchbook Journal

Each year, people buy millions of illustrated calendars. Calendar themes may range from cats to famous places. Think of a theme for a calendar that you would like to illustrate. Draw ideas for each month's illustration. Make notes about how you might match the illustration to the month.

Illustrated *Calendars*

Artist unknown. *Calendar Page,* 1827.

What details in this illustration tell you that it was made more than one hundred years ago?

Just as every author has a unique writing style, every illustrator has his or her own graphic style. An illustrator's **graphic style** is influenced by the media and techniques he or she uses. Current fads or trends may also influence an illustrator's style.

- Notice the illustration above and those in advertisements, publications, and product packaging. Identify any similarities that reflect current trends, such as illustrations using only contour drawings.
- Look for color trends in illustrations. One year, green may be the trendy color, or illustrators may choose to use only black and white.

Developing Graphic Style

Illustrators often spend years developing their own unique style. They look for trends to find a style that stands out from the crowd and yet fits in with the times.

Technique Tip

Making a Calendar Grid

Math skills come in handy when you need to create a calendar grid. A computer is a good medium to use in making such a grid. Each month may begin on a different day of the week. So you will need five rows of seven squares to make sure you can start each month on the correct day of the week.

Make and Illustrate a Calendar

Use what you have learned about illustration to create a calendar.

Materials

✓ 12 sheets of heavy white paper
✓ computer and printer
✓ white glue or glue stick
✓ Sketchbook Journal (optional)
✓ drawing and/or painting media
✓ paintbrush

1 Use a computer to create a calendar grid for each month. Print the grids to fit on the heavy paper, leaving room for an illustration.

2 Glue one calendar grid to each sheet of heavy paper.

3 Illustrate each month of the calendar with media of your choice. Use themes and sketches from your Sketchbook Journal.

Review and Reflect

- Describe the theme of your calendar illustrations.
- How does the media you chose reflect your calendar's theme?
- What message does each of your illustrations convey about the month they represent?
- Who might you give your calendar to as a gift? Why?

Cartoonist

Cartoonists are often the comics of the art world. Their drawings show ideas, make a point, or just make you laugh. A cartoonist may draw a single image or a complete comic strip that tells a story. A story told in pictures this way is a form of **visual narrative.** Cartoonists often sell their artworks to newspapers, magazines, advertisers, and greeting card companies.

Cartoonists use colored pencils, pencil, crayons, pen and ink, and other drawing media.

" I have to go, Maureen.....I think the world's stopped rotating..."

Ian Baker. *World's Stopped Rotating,* 2003.
Courtesy of the artist. © Ian Baker.

"I think it was an election year."

Danny Shanahan. *"I think it was an election year,"* 2000. Published in *The New Yorker,* July 14, 2000. © *The New Yorker* Collection 2000 Danny Shanahan from cartoonbank.com. All rights reserved.

What do you think was the artist's intended message of this political cartoon?

Editorial Cartooning

The job of an editorial cartoonist is different from that of a comic strip artist. An editorial cartoonist draws **political cartoons** to express opinions. Sometimes these cartoons make fun of their subject. Political cartoons often use **satire,** a form of humor that exposes a weakness or fault of the cartoon's subject. These cartoons often appear on the editorial pages of newspapers and magazines.

Many editorial cartoonists work for newspapers. They use lines and exaggeration to show their subjects. They often include animals or other objects as symbols in their artworks. Look on the editorial page of your local newspaper. Identify the shading technique the artist used.

Research

Some editorial cartoonists have won top journalism prizes. Do research about the history of editorial cartooning. What events and social issues led to editorial cartooning? Who were some of the pioneers in this field? Bring in examples of award-winning cartoons to share with the class.

THE FAR SIDE® BY GARY LARSON

© 1985 FarWorks, Inc. All Rights Reserved/Dist. by Creators Syndicate.

The Far Side® by Gary Larson © 1985 FarWorks, Inc. All Rights Reserved. Used with permission.

Exaggeration is common in all forms of humor.

Cartoonists find many ways to express ideas and create humor about people or characters. One common style is **caricature.** Caricature artists exaggerate a physical feature, such as the nose or ears. They may also show the subject involved in a hobby or favorite activity. The exaggerated features help the viewer recognize the person in a humorous way.

- Find examples of caricature in editorial cartoons or other drawings. Notice what physical feature of each character the cartoonist chose to focus on and how it affects your idea of the subject.
- Review what you have learned about altered proportion in Unit 2, Lesson 3. Altered proportion is a key to drawing caricatures.

Cartoons and Animals

People sometimes wonder what their pets or other animals might be thinking. Or they may wonder what the animals would say if they could talk. Cartoon artists often give human qualities to animals to create humor, such as the cartoon on this page. These cartoons can make people laugh or sometimes think about their own behavior.

Technique Tip

Choosing Media for Cartoons

As you decide what drawing medium to use for a cartoon, think about how to match the medium to your subject. For example, to draw a detailed scene or a person, choose a medium that makes thin lines. For a simple drawing with few lines, a medium that produces a thick line may be better.

Studio 2

Draw a Cartoon

Use what you have learned about cartooning to draw a cartoon based on a historical event.

Materials

✓ 12" × 18" white drawing paper
✓ drawing media

1 Think of a historical event that you would like to show in a cartoon. Show the event in a single cartoon or a cartoon strip.

2 Choose a medium and draw the event you chose. Include exaggeration or satire in your cartoon.

3 Use appropriate media to draw your cartoon. Include a caption.

Review and Reflect

- Tell what is happening in your cartoon. How did you use exaggeration?
- How does your portrayal of the characters or people compare to the actual characters?
- What is the message of your cartoon? How did you use humor to show it?
- Do you think readers will understand the meaning of your cartoon? Explain.

Photographer

Have you ever seen a professional **photographer** at work? Maybe you have seen one taking photographs at a wedding or sports event. There are many kinds of photographers, almost as many as there are objects and events to photograph. Some photograph fashions or products. Others travel the world to "shoot," or photograph, animals in the wild. An aerial photographer might stand atop a tall building or take photographs from an airplane to create a dramatic effect or to show a specific subject.

Photographers use special equipment such as this telephoto lens and tripod to get exactly the pictures they want.

Ansel Adams.
The Tetons-Snake River, 1942. Black-and-white photograph. National Archives and Records Administration, Records of the National Park Service.

Neville Elder. *Firemen on 9-11,* 2001. Color photograph.

Photojournalism

Photojournalists make visual records of history. They record news events around the world through photographs. They may use wide angles or different views to compose their images. These techniques help create dramatic effects and add to the photograph's visual story. Photojournalists are often under pressure to capture a fleeting moment on film. But they consider the composition of each photograph as they shoot.

While technical skills are most important, photojournalists must always be prepared. They never know when breaking news will need to be captured on film. They must be able to plan, think, and work quickly in the midst of unexpected and sometimes dangerous events.

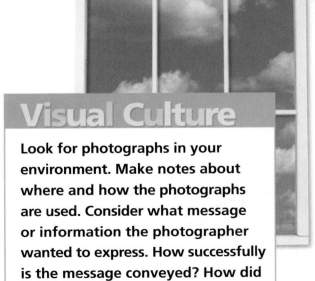

Visual Culture

Look for photographs in your environment. Make notes about where and how the photographs are used. Consider what message or information the photographer wanted to express. How successfully is the message conveyed? How did the artist use the elements of art and principles of design?

Photographic *Still Life*

Jan Groover. *Untitled,* 1979. Chromogenic color print, 16 by 20 inches. Edition of 3. JG#95.2.

Like painters, photographers often show still lifes.

Snapping pictures is only a part of being a photographer. Photographers also need to know about techniques in developing film into photographs. These techniques make printed images from what is recorded on film. Digital images, once downloaded to a computer, can be altered and printed using special paper and a photo printer.

- Most photographers learn how to work in a darkroom. Different chemicals and processes produce varied effects.
- More and more photographers are using digital cameras and technology. Does the photograph above appear to have been altered on a computer? Explain.

Photography and Technology

The first photograph was taken in 1827 and took eight hours to develop. Today film can be developed in as little as one hour or less. Current technology allows photographers to display and print images on a computer.

Technique Tip

Cropping Photographs

Cropping is a technique for editing photographs. Cropping can change the emphasis of a photograph or remove parts that take away from the main image or subject. Using a computer, save a copy of a photograph in one file and experiment with other versions. Crop each differently to see different views.

Studio 3

Create a Photo Collection

Use what you have learned about photography to create a photo exhibit with a theme that ties them together.

Materials

✓ camera
✓ ruler
✓ scissors ⚠️
✓ colored posterboard or construction paper
✓ glue stick
✓ display space

1 Choose a theme for your exhibit. Possible themes are people starting their day, dogs on walks, or interesting architectural details.

2 Compose several photographs using the elements of art and principles of design to illustrate your theme. Choose your favorites.

3 Crop any photographs as needed. Mount them on posterboard or construction paper. Display them.

Review and Reflect

- Describe your photo exhibit. What is the theme of the exhibit?
- How are all the photographs alike? How do they differ?
- What mood or feeling does your exhibit convey? What is a good title for the exhibit?
- How could you improve your exhibit?

Interior Designer

Interior designers plan the layout and design of rooms and buildings. These design artists try to create spaces that are both useful and attractive. Knowledge of **home fashions,** or items such as furniture, fabrics, and wall art, are important in this career. The designer matches these items to each owner's taste, needs, and budget. Some interior designers design commercial interiors such as banks, movie theaters, restaurants, or other buildings.

Interior designers use their knowledge of colors, shapes, space, and textures to work with their clients.

Philippe Starck. *Felix Restaurant.* Peninsula Hotel, Hong Kong.

Cecil Hayes. *African-American Research Library and Cultural Center,* 2002. Montgomery, AL.
Courtesy the Broward County Library.

Interior Design Skills

A career in interior design requires many art and design skills. These artists have a strong knowledge of the elements of art and principles of design. They use drawing skills to create **diagrams** for their clients. Clients get an idea of the designer's plan from these two-dimensional room layouts. Some designers create their diagrams by hand. Others use computer software to plan their designs. Their final product, though, is in three dimensions. Understanding the use of space and how the design of an area affects the way it will be used are important techniques of interior design.

Sketchbook Journal

Make a quick sketch of one room in your home as it is. Think of some changes that you think could improve the room, such as a new color scheme or furniture arrangement. Draw a new design. Make notes explaining why the new design is an improvement.

Identify repeated shapes and colors in this room design.

Interior designers use many techniques to influence how people will feel and act in a room. The kind of lighting in a room, for example, may affect how loudly people talk or how long they stay. One design element that strongly affects people is color. Review what you learned about color and color schemes in Unit 1, Lesson 8. Then notice how color is used in the indoor space shown above and in rooms in which you spend time.

- Notice the colors used in your school cafeteria, library, and classroom. Think about why those colors were chosen and how they affect you and others.
- Notice color schemes used in other public places, such as restaurants and stores. Would you change the colors in any of these places? Why or why not?

Other Elements

Interior designers also match flooring materials, furnishings, and artwork to the use of a room. They consider not only appearance and comfort, but also how much wear various materials can take.

Technique Tip

Furniture Cutouts
Interior design considers how to efficiently and effectively use the entire space of a room. An interior design diagram often shows furnishings in proportion. Measure furniture such as sofas and chairs. Then cut scale models out of graph paper. Use the cutouts to try different arrangements in a room design.

Design a Theme Room

Use what you have learned about interior design to draw a diagram of a room with a purpose and theme.

Materials

✓ sketch paper
✓ colored pencils
✓ graph paper
✓ ruler
✓ furniture cutouts (optional)

1 Choose a theme for your design. It can be a room in a home, such as a home theater, or a public space, such as a theme restaurant.

2 Think about how people would use the room. Draw several ideas for color schemes and furniture arrangements.

3 Use colored pencils to draw your final interior design on graph paper. Include notes about materials and furnishings.

Review and Reflect

- Describe the function and theme of the room you designed.
- How did you use the elements of art and principles of design to reflect the theme? Do these contribute to the room's function? Explain.
- How might a visitor to your room feel? What elements of your design contribute to this feeling?
- What was the most difficult part of designing your room? How did you solve the problem in a creative way?

Meet *the Artist*

Maya Lin

When Maya Lin was a college student, her professors told her that she had to choose between being an architect and being a sculptor. Lin enrolled as a student of architecture, but she kept taking classes in sculpture too. More than twenty years later, Lin is an award-winning architect and sculptor. Her artworks can be seen in cities across the United States. Each one reflects Lin's respect for the natural environment.

Maya Lin has focused on different art forms at different times in her career.

"I think art is wonderful because it's everything you've ever known and everything you've ever done."—MAYA LIN

Early Fame . . . and Controversy

Maya Lin is the daughter of two college professors. They moved to the United States from China ten years before she was born. Her family placed great value on education. In 1981, while Lin was still a student at Yale University, her design for a memorial honoring Vietnam veterans was chosen from more than fourteen hundred others in a national contest. While some war veterans protested Lin's design, wanting a more traditional sculpture, she won global fame and recognition. In spite of early protests, the *Vietnam Veterans Memorial* became the most visited public monument in the nation.

New Directions

Lin earned bachelor's and master's degrees in architecture. After designing the *Civil Rights Memorial*, Lin became interested in new forms of architecture and sculpture. She began designing what she calls topographic landscapes. *The Wave Field,* shown on page 250, is an example of this type of landscape.

In 1995, a film was made about Lin's career. *Maya Lin: A Strong, Clear Vision,* won the Academy Award for best documentary. Today, Lin continues to work as both an architect and a sculptor.

Talk About It

- Why do you think Lin chooses not to limit herself to one art form?

- How old was Lin when she designed the *Vietnam Veterans Memorial*?

The Life of Maya Lin

1945

1949
Lin's parents move from China to Ohio

1959
Maya Lin born in Athens, Ohio (April 14)

1960

Vietnam Veterans Memorial

A student at Yale University, Lin's design wins competition for the *Vietnam Veterans Memorial*

1975

1981

Lin earns Master of Architecture degree from Yale University

1986

1987
Lin opens a studio where she works on projects in art and architecture

1990

1989
Civil Rights Memorial, designed by Lin, dedicated in Montgomery, Alabama

(detail) *Civil Rights Memorial*

1995
Documentary film about Lin, *Maya Lin: A Strong, Clear Vision,* wins Academy Award

2000
Lin's book, *Boundaries,* is published

2005

Look *and Compare*

Two Approaches to Sculpture

As you have read in this book, art is a way of expressing ideas and feelings. The special way in which each artist changes ideas into images is what makes art fascinating. Both sculptures shown on page 271 were designed by American women in recent years. Note how the artists expressed their ideas in completely different ways.

No matter the style, artists' skills help them express their visions.

Abstract Sculpture

Maya Lin designed *Women's Table* to honor the women who have attended Yale since the university began to admit them. The granite table has a hole in the middle through which water runs. The tabletop is inscribed with numbers that begin with zero and increase to show the growing number of women who have studied at Yale. The sculpture is abstract. It does not show any images of women. Viewers must think about and interpret the sculpture to grasp its meaning.

Narrative Sculpture

Glenna Goodacre (1939–) designed *The Irish Memorial* to commemorate the Irish immigrants who came to America to escape famine in Ireland. Her sculpture uses lifelike figures to tell the story.

Both sculptures honor a group of people that have overcome hardships. But each artist expressed her ideas and feelings about these groups using different media and styles. How does each sculpture reflect the purpose for which it was designed? How do you think those honored by each sculpture might feel about the designs?

Maya Lin. *Women's Table,* 1993. Sterling Memorial Library, Yale University, New Haven, CT. Photo © Michael Marsland/Yale University.

Glenna Goodacre. *The Irish Memorial,* 2001. Bronze, 11 ½ by 35 feet. Philadelphia, PA.

Compare & Contrast

- Why do you think each artist chose the materials she did? How do these designs fit into their respective environments?

- If you were hiring an artist to design a sculpture, which of these two artists would you hire? Why?

Graphic Designer

What do an athletic shoe symbol or **logo,** a cereal box, a theme park sign, a movie poster, and the letters on this page have in common? They were all designed by graphic designers. **Graphic designers** are artists who create visual communications with images and lettering. Their works are everywhere. Many graphic designers specialize in one area, such as package design or advertising design.

Many graphic designers do early sketches by hand, and then complete their designs on a computer. Graphic designers are almost always part of a team that works together to produce a finished product.

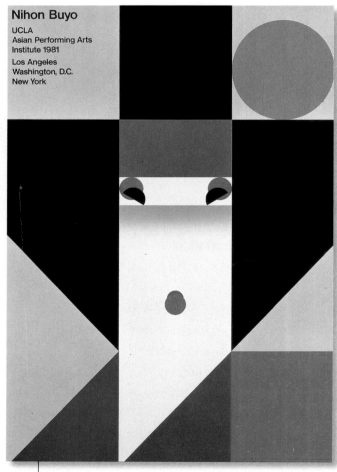

Nihon Buyo
UCLA
Asian Performing Arts
Institute 1981
Los Angeles
Washington, D.C.
New York

Ikko Tanaka. *Nihon Buyo,* 1981.
© Ikko Tanaka Archive.

Michael Bartalos. *Design Quarterly #166. Fiftieth Anniversary Issue.* © Michael Bartalos.

A Designer's Life

Graphic designers often work alone at a computer. What they do there may depend on other people involved in the project, such as writers, photographers, illustrators, and marketing experts. The graphic designer must understand information provided by all of these team members. Then he or she creates a design to communicate a message to an audience. The graphic designer may choose to use only images. Or colorful words may make up the design. Others may use a combination of these. How would you use images and words as a graphic designer?

Sketchbook Journal

Think of a concert or other local event that you enjoy. Make notes of ideas that you might use in an advertisement for the event. Include words and sketches to show what makes the event enjoyable. Note design components, such as color and typefaces that grab attention.

Ikko Tanaka. *Man and Writing,* 1981.
© Ikko Tanaka Archive.

Notice how the artist used color to create emphasis.

The work of graphic designers is all around you. You may not think about who designed a stop sign, for example, but someone made a career of doing so. Begin to notice graphic design everywhere you go. Look at signs, menus, logos, advertisements, publications, and more. Think about the elements of art each designer used to create each design.

- Look at the striking image created by Tanaka in *Man and Writing.* Notice how the image suggests both power and mystery.
- Study the logos of companies such as restaurants and automakers. Notice how the work of graphic designers helps convey the company's product or image. Think about what makes you remember the different designs.

Layout

Most graphic designers use computer programs to lay out their designs. A layout is the way the designer arranges text and images. The placement of these depends on the message. Perhaps a large word grabs your attention. Or maybe a bold, simple image catches your eye. Whatever the layout, if you noticed it, the designer did his or her job!

Technique Tip

Type Design

Computer drawing software allows most anyone to design type styles or fonts. You can design an entire font, or style of letters. You can also draw only the letters you need to spell out an important word in a graphic design. Experiment with creating unique fonts on a computer. Use a color scheme as you create letters.

Studio 5

Design a Sports Poster

Use what you have learned about graphic design to create a poster advertising a sports event.

Materials

✓ computer with drawing software (optional)
✓ printer (optional)
✓ pencil and 12" × 18" drawing paper
✓ posterboard or large paper
✓ tempera paints and brushes
✓ colored markers or pencils

1 Think of a real or imaginary sports event to advertise on a poster. Use a computer or pencil and paper to create your layout.

2 Include the name of the event, date, time, and place.

3 Add color and details using the medium of your choice.

Review and Reflect

- Describe the elements of art and principles of design in your poster.
- Why did you choose the images and colors that you used? How did you decide type sizes and styles?
- Does the mood of your poster reflect the sports event? Explain.
- What about your poster makes viewers want to read it?

Industrial Designer

The people who designed the first wheel were **industrial designers,** but that is not what they were called. They saw a need for a new device. They started thinking about what it would look like and how it could be made. Today's industrial designers work with scientists and engineers. These artists determine the form and appearance of products such as cars, appliances, and toys that are mass-produced in factories.

Michael Graves. *"MG32"* design, Electric kettle, 2001. Produced by Alessi s.p.a.–Italy.

Car designers start with drawings and eventually build full-size models from their best designs.

Michael Graves. (Detail) *"MG32"* design.

Tyson Boles. *Pan.*
Electric lamp design.

Notice the effects
created by the light
shining through
this lamp's design.

Industrial Design Skills

New technologies change how products
are made and used. Industrial designers stay
up to date on new materials and processes
to make products better. They spend a lot of
time drawing and making models to solve
problems. For example, how do you make
a product both strong and lightweight?
Successful industrial designers attack these
challenges creatively. They may invent
new products or "rethink" existing ones.
Most industrial designers work in teams.
These teams may include other designers,
engineers, researchers, and sales experts.

Sketchbook Journal

**Notice products or items
around you that you think are
well designed. Draw some of
these objects, and make notes
about what makes the design
better than other versions of
the same product. Take notes
on materials, colors, and
features that make them
attractive or easy to use.**

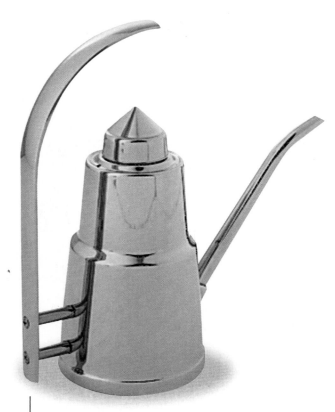

Liliana Bonomi. *"Elaios" Oil Server.* Stainless steel, 8 by 3 ⅓ inches. Courtesy of Serafino Zani, Italy.

How would you describe the style of this product?

Industrial designers design products that work well and are easy and safe to use. But style is often what sells. Most designers combine current trends with their own ideas.

- Bonomi's oil server includes geometric and organic shapes. The design is sleek and modern with a smooth, shiny texture.

- Notice how the oversized handle and spout balance each other visually. These features also provide a sense of rhythm and motion.

Postmodern and Classic Styles

Modern style refers to artworks of the late nineteenth and early twentieth centuries. Modern artists used new technologies such as structural iron, steel, and glass as inspiration. They focused more on function rather than decorative features.

The **Postmodern** style followed modernism. Artworks of this style often combine traditional designs with those of the popular culture. These might include simple decorative shapes, sleek finishes, and even humor. Liliana Bonomi's oil server is an example of Postmodern style.

The **Classic** style has come to mean perfection of form, much like the sculptures of ancient Greece. This style focuses on harmony and unity in useful and attractive designs.

Technique Tip

Drawing to Scale

When you design a product, you may find it helpful to draw to scale. For example, it would be difficult to draw a full-scale car. So you would draw it on a smaller scale. Consider drawing the car's door handle or other parts in normal scale to show detail. Inset these details to provide more information about your design.

Studio 6

Redesign a Tool or Appliance

Use what you have learned about industrial design to create an improved design for a common product.

Materials

- ✓ sketchpad or paper
- ✓ pencil
- ✓ colored pencils
- ✓ markers

1 Choose a product that you use, such as a tool or appliance, that you could redesign.

2 Draw ideas for a new, improved design for the product. Consider current trends in styles, safety, and product function.

3 Use colored pencils and/or markers to draw your final design. Include notes about materials to be used in making the product.

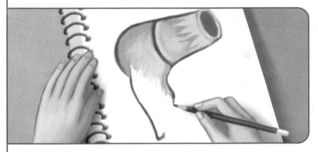

Review and Reflect

- Describe the original product's design and your new design of the product.
- How are the shapes and forms of your product different from other products like it?
- What does your new design say about the meaning and function of the product?
- In what ways is your design an improvement over the original design?

Landscape Designer

Landscape designers are artists who use nature as their medium. Their work can be seen in public spaces such as parks, grounds of buildings, and even along roadsides. Landscape designers use trees, flowers, grasses, stones, water, and the shape of the land itself. Some landscapes are made simply to look at. Others are designed and created for a specific purpose, such as golf courses and theme parks.

Frederick Law Olmsted joined forces with landscape architect Calvert Vaux to design New York City's 840-acre Central Park. The designers' first and foremost consideration was nature. Vaux once said, "Nature first, second, and third—architecture after a while."

Topographical maps and other data help designers plan landscapes.

Frederick Law Olmsted and Calvert Vaux, landscape architects. *Central Park,* 1859–1863. New York City.

Artist unknown. *Japanese Tea Garden.* Golden Gate Park, San Francisco, CA.

Before the Design

When you look at an area, what appeals to your eye? A landscape design is a **visual composition,** an arrangement of objects in a given space. Because nature is the starting point, landscape designers must work with the natural setting. They note topography, or how land rises and falls. They consider the soil conditions, patterns of sunlight and shade. They also consider wind direction, drainage, what is nearby, and how birds or other wildlife may be affected. Finally, they think about how people will use the space.

Landscape designers determine which plants will grow in a specific climate. They often plan water features, such as ponds and fountains, and how these will work with the surroundings and overall design. The designer then formalizes the plan on paper.

Sketchbook Journal

Look carefully at physical features of landscape designs in your community. Draw a few of these spaces from a bird's-eye view. Take notes on how the design is laid out and balanced and whether it works with the natural environment.

Studio 7 Setup
Home *Garden Design*

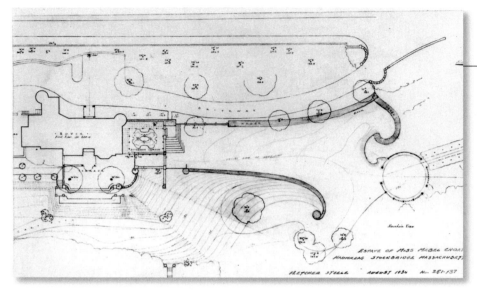

Fletcher Steele. *Plan of South Lawn, Naumkeag Gardens, Stockbridge, MA.* Courtesy of Fletcher Steele Archives, SUNY ESF, F. Franklin Moon Library.

What parts of landscape composition can you identify in this design?

What grows well where you live? Different styles of landscape design have developed in different countries, climates, and time periods. Landscape designs vary greatly depending on whether you live in Maine or Florida, Arizona or Oregon. Notice the features of the landscape design plan above. Then look closely at landscape designs where you live.

- Pay attention to what kinds of trees, shrubs, and flowers you see repeated in many landscapes. Think about why the designer chooses specific plants.
- Notice how landscapes are laid out and what features are common.

Using the Picture Plane

Remember that all landscape designs start as sketches. Landscape designers represent complex, three-dimensional spaces on a **picture plane,** or the flat surface of the paper. This allows them to show the exact placement of plants and other design elements such as trees, fountains, and flowers from a bird's-eye view.

Technique Tip

Using Symbols

Landscape designers use symbols to show trees, shrubs, flowerbeds, fountains, and other items in their designs. Think about how each would look from a bird's-eye view. Experiment with different symbols that you could use for the features in a landscape design. You can cut out symbols from paper or posterboard and draw around them on your design.

Draw a Landscape Design

Use what you have learned about landscape design to draw a design for a new park in your community.

Materials

- ✓ sketchpad
- ✓ pencil
- ✓ graph paper
- ✓ symbol shapes (optional)
- ✓ colored pencils and watercolors
- ✓ paintbrushes and water container
- ✓ ruler

1 Suppose that you have been hired to design a new park that will cover one city block. Draw ideas for a landscape design.

2 Use colored pencils to draw your final design on graph paper. Add a splash of color with watercolors.

3 Include a key explaining any symbols you use in your design. Also include notes about plant types and materials.

Review and Reflect

- Describe the location of your park and the design elements you included.
- How did you make your design fit the climate and setting?
- How will people use the park you have designed?
- What features of your design would draw visitors to the park? Why?

Lesson 8

Art Teacher

What is it about your favorite teacher that makes him or her special? Somehow that teacher gets you to think about or see the world in a new way. An **art teacher** helps students understand and participate in a world of images and ideas. Art teachers give students new ways to view art, to think about art, to talk about art, and to make art. But you already know that!

Summer camps, private art schools, and museums often have art teachers.

Art teachers spend time outside the classroom observing artworks and planning lessons.

LESSON PLANS

CLASS	MONDAY
Gesture Drawing	a. pencils or charcoal, white paper
	b. 30-second drawing exercises
	c. multiple student models (5 min. each)
	TUESDAY
Shar...	a. oil pastels, white...

Art Skills and Teaching Skills

You have to know what you are talking about to teach anything. Art teachers need a broad knowledge of art and art processes to share with their students. Like all teachers, they must be good communicators. They are also good **motivators** who encourage students to learn by doing. An art teacher may create his or her own **curriculum,** a set of lessons and projects used to teach a subject. He or she creates lesson plans based on a set of standards. These art standards include both national and state objectives for teaching art.

Because not everyone learns the same way, teachers use various methods, called **teaching strategies,** to help all students enjoy learning about art. For example, some students are visual learners. These students may learn best through observation or visual images.

Research

To learn about art teachers in your school and community, find places that offer art classes, such as museums, schools, and colleges. Talk to art teachers in your school or community to learn about their jobs. Discover what they like about their career and why they chose it.

What opportunities might a career as an art teacher provide?

Every art teacher has his or her own way of teaching. Good teachers create a style.

- Think about art classes that you have taken, especially classes that you found interesting and fun. What made those classes work? For example, maybe the teacher asked questions that sparked a good discussion. Maybe you did a lot of hands-on activities.
- Recall a time when you had difficulty in an art class. Helping students is an important part of an art teacher's job.

Planning Ahead

Teachers spend a good deal of time preparing the lessons that they want to teach. Before class, an art teacher chooses what material to cover and what students should know about it. Next, the teacher decides what kinds of information and

activities will interest students and get across the ideas. Teachers usually plan several different ways to teach the material. Finally, the teacher gathers all needed materials, models, and examples.

Technique Tip

Practice Teaching

Even if you know how to do something very well, it may be challenging to teach it to someone else. Practice each step that you plan to teach, both in what you do and what you say. Try out steps or demonstrations with a new learner, or someone who knows almost nothing about what you are going to teach. You may be amazed at what happens.

Plan and Teach an Art Lesson

Use what you have learned about teaching art to plan and teach an art lesson.

Materials

✓ writing paper and pencil
✓ materials and models needed for your lesson

1 Choose a favorite art process or project to share with your classmates. Pick something you know and do well.

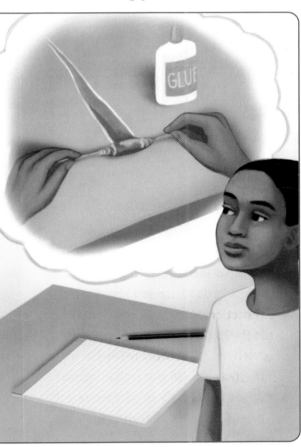

2 Write a lesson plan that outlines key ideas and steps. Prepare models or demonstrations. Gather needed materials.

Materials list:
colored paper
knitting needle
glue
string

3 Present your lesson to the class. Be prepared to answer questions and to provide help. Provide a display of students' artworks.

Review and Reflect

• What was the main idea of the lesson you taught?
• How did you choose what information and models to present?
• Why would your lesson be a valuable part of an art curriculum?
• What did you like best and least about your lesson? What would you change if you taught it again?

Design a Building Facade

Michael Graves. *Humana Building,* 1982. Louisville, KY. Photograph courtesy of Mary Ann Sullivan, Bluffton College, Bluffton OH.

Plan

You read about architecture in Unit 3. You also read how artist Maya Lin combines sculpture and architecture in her designs. Architect Michael Graves (1934–) used his knowledge to design the Humana Building. The **facade,** or front, of a building is the part that people notice first. For that

reason, architects give careful attention to the facades of buildings they design. Look closely at the facade of Graves's design.

- Graves is a Postmodern architect. The tripartite, or three-part, design of the facade is common in Postmodern skyscrapers. What other qualities of Postmodernism do you see in the facade of the *Humana Building?*
- What feeling or mood does the facade convey? What do you think Graves wanted to express through his design?
- How could you use your knowledge of art to help you design a facade? What style would you use?

Use what you have learned about design and architecture to design a building facade.

Sketchbook Journal

Think of a kind of building that you would like to design, such as a movie theater, planetarium, or museum. Then draw some ideas for a facade for the building. Experiment with ways to add interest to the facade. Make notes about what materials might be used to construct the building.

Materials

- ✓ facade design from Sketchbook Journal (optional)
- ✓ 12" × 16" white drawing paper
- ✓ pencil
- ✓ white posterboard
- ✓ posterboard or paper scraps
- ✓ ruler
- ✓ scissors ⚠
- ✓ glue

Create

1 Decide on a final design for your facade. Use a pencil and a ruler to draw the design on drawing paper.

2 Cut the pieces you need to "build" your facade from posterboard or paper scraps. Use a ruler and a pencil to draw the shape of each piece before cutting it out with scissors.

3 Glue the pieces of posterboard on top of one another to build your facade. Use additional pieces to add dimension to your design.

4 Score parts of the facade with the tip of the scissors to create texture and pattern. Is your design balanced?

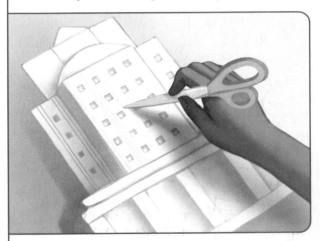

Reflect

- What problems did you have while completing your facade? How did you solve them?
- How did you use style to help you express an idea or a mood?
- What did you learn about designing a building facade?
- Talk to a classmate about the project. How are your facades the same? How are they different?

Unit 6 *Review*

Vocabulary Review

A Match each art term below with its definition.

> caricature   illustration
> visual narrative   digital
> applied arts   technology
> Classic   Postmodern
> crafts   logo
> picture plane

1. works of art created by hand
2. artworks meant to be used
3. images that tell a story
4. computer, graphics tablet, and scanner
5. a style that focuses on harmony and unity in useful and attractive designs
6. symbol that identifies a company or group
7. portrait with exaggerated features
8. a style that combines traditional and modern features
9. the area of a sheet of paper that is used for drawing
10. an artwork that visually tells about a text

Artists and Their Careers

B Match each artist and artwork in the box with the careers below.

> Glenna Goodacre, *The Irish Memorial*
> Ian Baker, *World's Stopped Rotating*
> Michael Graves, *Humana Building*
> Neville Elder, *Firemen on 9-11*
> Michael Bartalos, *Design Quarterly #166*
> Arthur Rackham, *There is Almost Nothing That Has Such a Keen Sense of Fun . . .*
> Liliana Bonomi, *"Elaios" Oil Server*
> Frederick Law Olmsted, *Central Park*

1. Illustrator
2. Landscape Designer
3. Industrial Designer
4. Architect
5. Graphic Designer
6. Cartoonist
7. Photojournalist
8. Sculptor

Glenna Goodacre

Frederick Law Olmsted

Respond to Art

C Look at each of the four photographs representing art careers. Then choose the art term below that best matches the letters in each photograph.

Art Terms

1. interior designer
2. landscape designer
3. layout
4. developing techniques
5. home fashions
6. graphic designer
7. photojournalist
8. picture plane

Unit 6 *Review*

Write About Art

Compare and Contrast

D Look back at the artworks in this unit. Choose two artworks from the same lesson to compare and contrast. Copy the Venn diagram below and fill it in. Use the completed diagram to help you write an essay comparing and contrasting the two artworks.

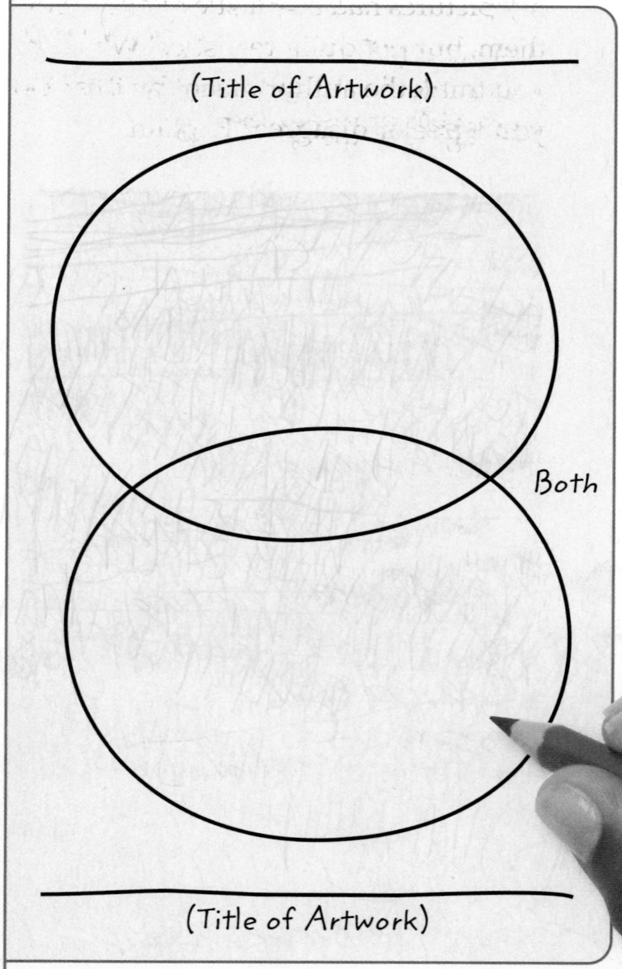

(Title of Artwork)

Both

(Title of Artwork)

Your Studio Work

E Answer these questions in your Sketchbook Journal or on a separate sheet of paper.

1. What career or careers in this unit interested you the most? Explain.
2. What problems did you have as you tried the skills and techniques used by each career? How did you solve them? What will you do differently next time?
3. Which artworks inspired your own art-making process?
4. Choose one artwork to keep in your portfolio. Tell why you chose it.

Put It All Together

Daniel Minter. *Untitled*, 1994. Illustration from *The Footwarmer and the Crow*, written by Evelyn Coleman.

F Discuss or write about Minter's artwork using the four steps for critically viewing artwork.

1. **Describe** What does this artwork show? Describe the figures and objects and their environment.
2. **Analyze** What media and techniques did Minter use to create the artwork? What clues help you figure this out?
3. **Interpret** What do you think is the meaning or message of this artwork? What is the mood? What do you think *The Footwarmer and the Crow* is about?
4. **Judge** American artist Daniel Minter (1961–) has said that the author of *The Footwarmer and the Crow* "thought that my pictures had a realistic quality about them, but not dully realistic." What do you think the author meant by this? Do you agree or disagree? Explain.

Artist Daniel Minter has had jobs as an illustrator and as a graphic designer.

> "I felt that my illustrations were particularly good for the subject of the book . . . because they . . . have a kind of quality about them that is really narrative and clear." —DANIEL MINTER

Elements *of Art*

The elements of art are the basic parts and symbols of an artwork.

Line

A **line** is a continuous mark made by a moving point. Lines vary in width, length, direction, color, and degree of curve. Artists use line in many ways, for example, to define a space, create a pattern, or show movement.

Henri Matisse. *The Horse, the Rider, and the Clown, Plate V from the Jazz Series*, 1947.

Edvard Munch. *The Scream*, 1893.

Shape

A **shape** is an enclosed area of space, often defined by line. Shapes are two-dimensional, or flat, but can be made to look like solid three-dimensional objects. Some shapes are geometric, such as a rectangle or circle. Others are organic, having an irregular outline.

Form

A **form** is an object with three dimensions—height, width, and depth. Like shapes, forms can be geometric or organic.

Henry Moore. *Two-Piece Reclining Figure: Points*, 1969–1970.

Space

Space is the area around, above, between, inside, or below objects. Positive space is the area occupied by an object. Negative space is the empty area surrounding objects. Artists vary positive and negative space to imply size and distance.

Auguste Rodin. *The Cathedral*, 1955.

Value

Value refers to the lightness or darkness of a color. A light value, such as light pink, is a tint. A dark value, such as dark red, is a shade. Artists show transitions between different values to create depth or suggest a mood.

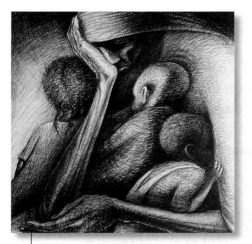

John Biggers. *The Cradle*, 1950.

Color

Color is the appearance of an object created by the characteristic of light it reflects and absorbs. A red object, for example, reflects red light and absorbs all other colors.

Diana Ong. *Beachcombers*, 1994.

Texture

Texture refers to the way a surface feels to the touch (tactile texture) or how it appears through the sense of vision (visual texture). Artists work one or both types of texture into their artworks to help viewers understand a surface quality.

Deborah Butterfield. *Horse #2–85*, 1985.

Principles *of Design*

The principles of design are guidelines that artists use to organize the elements of art in a composition.

Balance

Balance refers to the way the elements of art are arranged to create a sense of stability and equal visual weight. An artwork has balance if no one part visually overpowers another.

Artist unknown. *Eskimo Mask.*

Emphasis

Emphasis in an artwork is the sense of importance given to any one part of the composition. Artists add emphasis when they want to draw attention to a certain object or idea.

Andrew Wyeth. *The Chambered Nautilus,* 1956.

Proportion

Proportion refers to how the parts of an artwork relate to each other in size. An artist painting a portrait, for example, may keep in mind the size relationship of the nose to the face.

Artist unknown. *Nefertiti,* ca. 1365 B.C.

Pattern

Pattern is the repeated use of an element, such as line, shape, or color.

Artist unknown, Persian. *Panel of mosaic tilework,* 14th or 15th century.

Franz Marc. *The Monkey (Frieze),* 1911.

Unity

Unity is the quality of wholeness achieved when the separate parts of an artwork work well together. An artwork with unity often shows repeated elements, such as the frequent use of a shape.

Rhythm

Rhythm is a sense of movement in a composition created by the regular repetition of an element. Rhythm in an artwork can appear vibrant and active or calm.

Victor Vasarely. *Vega-Nor,* 1969.

Variety

Variety refers to the combination of different elements in an artwork. Artists energize their compositions by varying patterns, shapes, and colors. They strive to strike a balance between unity and variety.

Joseph Cornell. *Box with Objects,* 1941.

Think Safety

Read these safety rules and be sure to follow them when you create artworks.

1. Keep art materials away from your face to prevent eye irritation and skin rashes.

2. Do not breathe chalk dust or art sprays. These materials can be harmful to your lungs.

3. If you are allergic to an art material, notify your teacher before the project begins.

4. If you experience an allergic reaction to any art materials, stop using the materials immediately and notify your teacher.

5. Read the labels on art materials and look for the word *nontoxic*. This label tells you the materials are safe to use.

6. If you use a sharp-pointed object, such as a clay tool or scissors, point it away from your body. Point these objects away from other students, as well.

7. If you spill paint or other art materials on the floor, clean it up right away. It is unsafe to walk on a wet or cluttered floor.

8. Use only *new* meat trays and egg cartons as art materials. Used ones may carry harmful bacteria.

9. After you finish an artwork, wash your hands with soap and water.

Technique Handbook

Drawing with Crayon and Oil Pastels

1 Use the tip of a crayon or edge of the oil pastel to make a variety of lines, such as straight, curved, wavy, and cross-hatched. Draw short lines or dots of different colors side-by-side to create an Impressionist effect.

2 Peel the paper off the crayon or oil pastel and use the side to draw thick lines. Break the tool in half to reduce line width.

3 Press down firmly for bright colors. Press lightly for soft colors. Mix colors by putting one on top of another and blending them with your fingers or a tissue. Add a small amount of black to make a darker shade. Shade forms gradually from dark to light.

Drawing with Chalk Pastels

1 Use the tip of the chalk pastel to make a variety of lines. Practice drawing vertical, horizontal, and diagonal lines. Create broken lines by periodically lifting the chalk from the page.

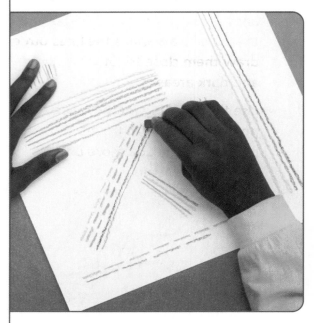

2 Use the side of the chalk to draw thick lines. Apply varying degrees of pressure to increase or decrease line quality.

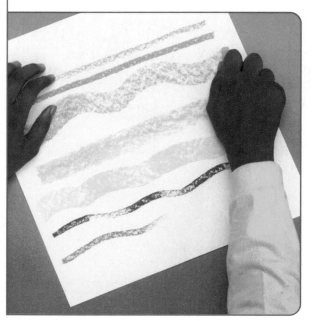

3 Mix colors by putting one color on top of another. Blend colors with a tissue, shading stump, or tortillon.

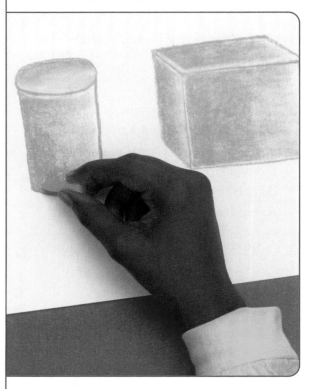

4 Use a kneaded eraser or an eraser of similar quality to add highlights.

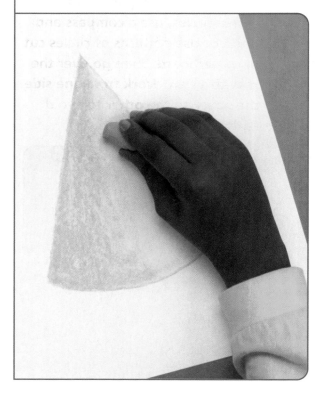

Drawing with Pen and Ink

1 Select a pen and drawing paper. Technical pens have different sized tips, or nibs, which allow you to draw lines of varying width. Ballpoint pens create crisp, clean lines. Choose smooth paper when working with ink. Rough paper can absorb ink quickly and give your drawing an uneven look.

2 Draw your design in pencil first. To create circles, use a compass and a pencil, or use patterns of circles cut from posterboard. Then go over the lines with a pen. Work from one side of the paper to the other to avoid smearing ink.

3 Shade forms with one or more of the following methods:

- Use a ruler to draw a series of parallel lines that get closer together. These lines will create a light-to-dark effect.

- Try cross-hatching. Draw parallel lines. Then add a layer of lines going the other way. Space the lines out or draw them close together for light and dark areas.

- Use the stippling method. Draw points or dots with the tip of the pen. Gradually add more dots to create darker values.

Creating a Contour Drawing

1 Place your drawing tool at the top of the paper and draw the contour lines of an object. Draw slowly to record the inside and outside folds, wrinkles, and creases as you see them. To create a continuous line, keep your hand and forearm in fluid motion and do not lift the drawing tool from the paper.

2 To create a blind contour drawing, cover your drawing paper with another sheet of paper and do not watch your progress. To create a modified contour drawing, allow yourself to look at the drawing from time to time to correct proportions.

Creating a Gesture Drawing

1 Notice the movement, pose, shape, weight, and form of a figure, preferably in action. Draw the figure using quick, rhythmic, scribbling sketches for one to three minutes. Draw geometric shapes to quickly capture the different forms that make up the human figure, such as an oval for the head and a cylinder shape for the neck.

2 Add details by showing dark areas, light areas, and gesture lines that contour around parts of a figure in action. Draw on large newsprint with charcoals, pastels, chalks, felt-tip pens, and other drawing media.

Making a Papier-Mâché Mask

1 Create the armature, or framework, for the mask. Cut out the shape of the mask from tagboard, posterboard, or another pliable material.

2 Glue or tape pieces of scrap cardboard, newspaper, or foam core to the armature to make the facial features stand out from the surface.

3 Tear and soak newspaper strips and/or paper towels in papier-mâché paste. Apply the strips, one over the other, to build up the surface of the armature, allowing each layer to dry. Add paper towels as the final two or three layers for a smooth surface. Use soft tissue paper soaked in papier-mâché paste to form eyes, eyebrows, and other features.

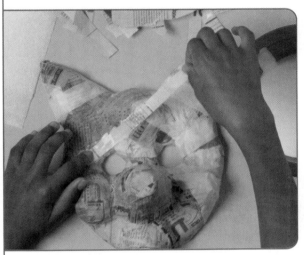

4 Allow the papier mâché to dry before applying paint. For best results, use acrylic-based paint. Or apply a water-soluble sealant to the dry surface for tempera paint. Add final details with yarn, raffia, beads, metallic foils, or other found objects.

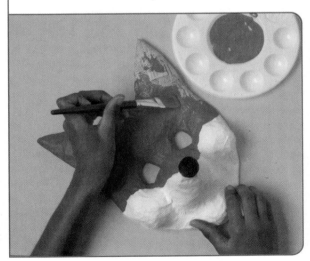

Painting with Tempera or Acrylic Paint

1 To mix a tint, begin with white paint and add a dot of colored paint. Continue adding color until you get the tint you want. To mix a shade, start with a color. Add a small amount of black paint and mix the two together. Avoid using too much black.

2 Dip the bristles of your paintbrush into the paint. Push down on the paintbrush for thick lines and use the tip for thin lines. Hold the brush at different angles to vary your lines.

3 Clean your paintbrush every time you switch colors. Dip the brush in water and wipe it on the side of the water container. Blot the brush on a paper towel before charging with the next color.

4 When finished, wash your paintbrush with warm, soapy water. Rinse the brush and blot it on a towel. Put the paintbrush into a jar, bristles up.

Painting with Watercolor

1 Prepare paints by brushing a large drop of water onto each color of paint. For best results, use watercolor paper for your compositions.

2 Practice mixing colors as they appear on the color wheel. Begin with a light color, such as yellow, and add a small amount of a darker color, such as blue. To create tints, add water. Water allows the white paper to show through the paint. To create shades, add a dot of black.

3 Plan a white space in your composition by creating a resist with a white crayon or white oil pastel. Then use a wet-wash to create sky and ground areas. Wet a broad brush and paint over your paper with clear water. Charge your brush with a color and pull the brush horizontally across the top. Work your way down to the horizon line without recharging your brush. Rinse the brush and repeat with a second color. Lift your paper vertically to allow the wet wash to blend.

4 Allow your wet wash to dry before you paint details, such as boats, rafts, a dock, or birds. Use watercolor paints, crayons, or oil pastels for the details. When the painting is dry, create highlights by scraping some paint away with a scraping tool.

Making a Monoprint

1 Cover a sheet of paper or a hard, slick surface with acrylic paint. Use a pencil or pen to draw a design into the paint.

2 Place a sheet of clean paper on top of your design. Smooth it down gently with your hands. Carefully peel the paper off, known as "pulling the print," and let the paint dry.

Making a Relief Print

1 Use a pencil to draw a design on material such as a slab of clay or a clean meat tray. Cover a roller, or brayer, with water-based printers' ink or acrylic paint. Roll the ink or paint evenly over the design.

2 Place a clean sheet of paper on top of your design. Rub the paper gently with your hands. Carefully pull the print and let the ink or paint dry.

Making a Stamp Print

1 Cut a shape from a material such as cardboard or a clean meat tray. Attach a piece of twisted masking tape to the back of the shape to create a handle.

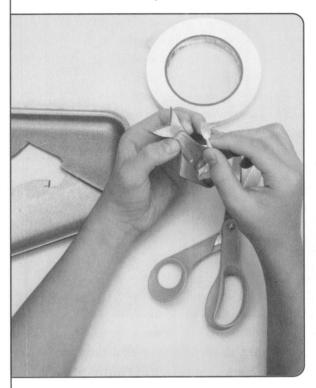

2 Use a brayer to roll a thin layer of printing ink or acrylic paint onto a printing tray or other flat surface.

3 Dip the face of the printing block or stamp into the ink or acrylic paint. Carefully, but firmly, press the stamp onto a sheet of paper. Lift the stamp to see the print.

Making a Collage

1 Decide on an idea or theme for your collage. Then collect what you will need. Cut out and tear shapes from colored papers and fabrics.

2 Arrange the paper and fabric pieces on a sheet of construction paper. Move them around until you find an arrangement that you like. Be sure to fill the construction paper background.

3 Glue the pieces, one at a time, to the background. Add found objects to create texture and enhance your design.

Working with Clay

Setup

When working with clay, cover your desk or work area with a plastic mat or canvas. Prepare any unwedged clay by wedging it. To wedge clay, take a large lump of it and thump it down on the work surface. Press the clay with the palms of your hands, turn it over, and press into it again. Keep pressing the clay until it has no air bubbles.

Forming a Pinch Pot

1 Make a small ball of clay and place it in the palm of your hand.

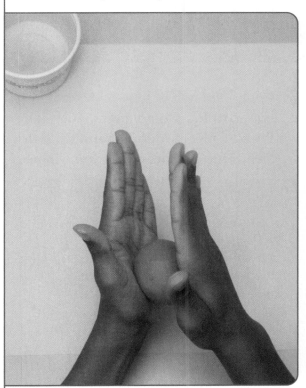

2 Press your thumb into the middle of the ball. Pinch it with your fingers.

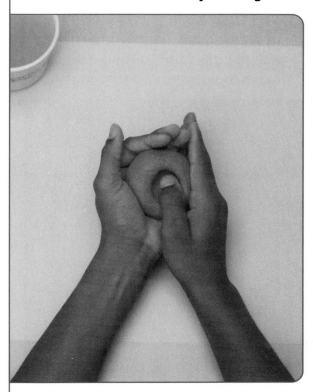

3 Start pinching at the bottom and then move up and out. Keep turning the ball as you pinch.

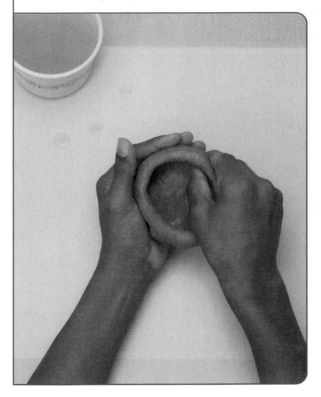

Using the Slab Method

1 Use a rolling pin to roll out a piece of wedged clay between two sticks. Roll the clay until it is approximately one-half inch thick.

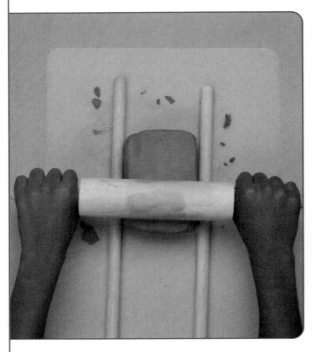

2 Cut out slabs for the bottom and sides of a container using a plastic knife.

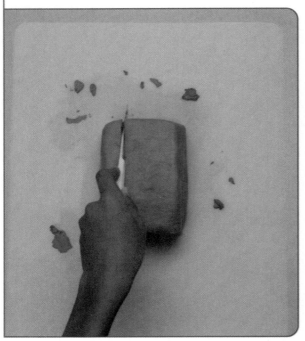

3 Use a moist toothbrush, toothpick, or plastic fork to create score marks. These rough grooves make it easier to join one piece of clay to another.

4 Apply slip, a mixture of clay and water, to the scored edges. Then join the slab pieces together and smooth any irregular places with your fingers.

Using the Coil Method

1 Begin with a flat and round slab as the base. Score the edges of your base.

2 Make a coil, or rope, of clay by rolling the clay back and forth between your hands and the work surface. Start rolling in the middle and move toward the edges.

3 Score each coil and apply slip to the coils and base.

4 Wind the coils into a form. Cut extra coils into pieces to form handles and other parts for your form. Score them and apply slip before you press them in place.

Making a Repoussé

1 Cut a sheet of metal foil made of aluminum or copper. Place tape around the edges of the metal for safety.

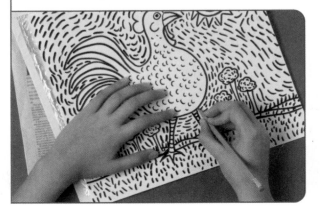

2 Draw a design on paper that will fit the size of the foil.

3 Place the foil on a soft pad, such as an old magazine or stack of newspapers. Use a blunt pencil to transfer your drawing to the foil.

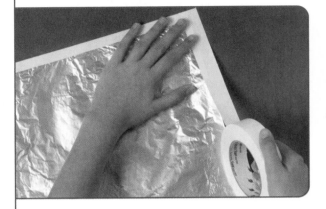

4 Remove the paper design and deepen the outline in the foil using craft sticks or the eraser end of a pencil.

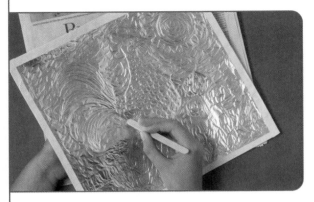

5 Turn the foil over and deepen the other shapes to make them stand out from the front side.

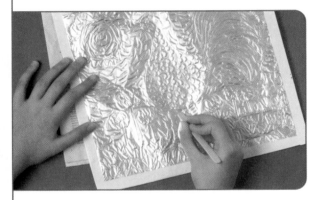

6 Brush waterproof ink or black shoe polish over the foil design. When the ink is dry, lightly buff, or rub, the raised surfaces with steel wool or a dry paper towel. Mount your repoussé on wood or heavy cardboard. Use acrylic spray to protect the artwork.

Weaving

1 Cut a piece of cardboard to make a square or rectangular loom. Use a ruler to draw lines one-half inch from the top and from the bottom. Then make a mark every one-fourth inch or so along the lines. Draw slanted lines from the edge of the cardboard to the marks. Cut along the slanted lines to make "teeth."

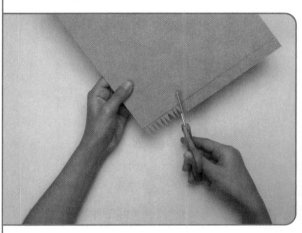

2 Next, create a warp. Make a loop in one end of a piece of yarn. Hook the loop around the first "tooth" at the top of the loom. Then take the yarn down to the bottom of the loom. Hook it around the first "tooth" there. Take the yarn back up to the second "tooth" at the top, hook it, and so on. Keep wrapping until the loom is filled with warp threads, or vertical lines of yarn.

3 Finally, weave the weft. Tie yarn through a hole in a narrow craft stick. Start at the bottom center of the loom. Weave toward one edge by going over and under the warp threads. When you get to the last thread, loop the craft stick around it and start weaving back in the other direction. Keep weaving, over and under, until the loom is covered. Unhook and remove the weaving from the loom. Tie any loose end pieces.

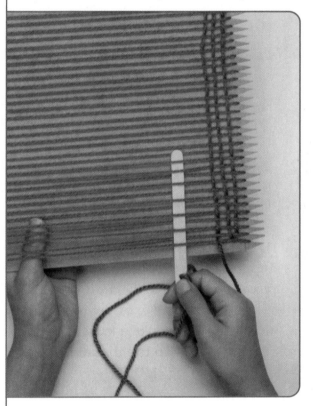

Making Stitchery

1 Select a needle. A crewel needle, used for embroidery, is short and has a long eye. A blunt needle, used for weaving, is a big needle with a dull point. A darner is a long needle with a big eye. It is used with thick threads, such as yarn. Never use a sharp needle without the help of an adult.

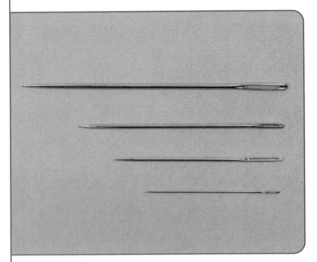

2 Thread the needle by dampening your fingers and pinching one end of the thread to flatten it. Push the flattened end through the eye of the needle and pull it through. Make a knot at the other end to keep the thread from coming through cloth.

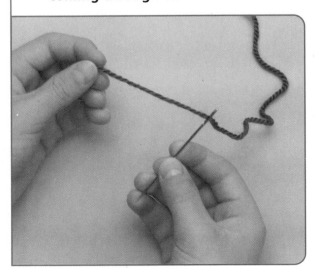

3 Start a stitch on the back of the cloth. Push the needle through and pull the thread up until the knot stops it. Continue pushing and pulling until you have finished your stitching. Finally, push the needle and thread through to the back. Make two small stitches next to each other and push the needle under these two stitches. Pull the thread through, knot it, and cut it off.

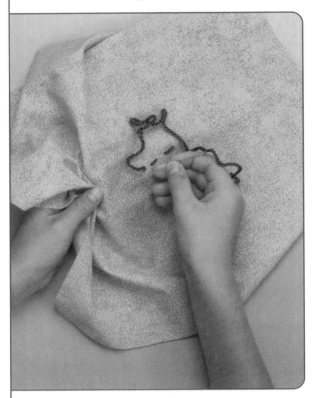

Drawing and Painting on a Computer

1 Select a new document from a drawing or painting software program. Practice using the drawing tools, such as thick and thin lines, shapes, paint, spray, eraser, and fill, as well as the text tool. Shade basic shapes to create forms. Create contour and gesture drawings of objects or a classmate. Fill the screen with your experimental designs.

2 Choose one of your practice designs or create a new design. Using the program's drawing tools, add form, color, texture, and value to your design. A graphics tablet and stylus may be used in place of a mouse. Repeat certain elements of your design. Add a background by scanning a design you created or using the fill and gradient patterns in your software program.

3 Use the text tool to incorporate a phrase or message around the edges, in the foreground or background. Use your imagination to help make your text message stand out.

List *of* Artists and Artworks

Unknown Artists

Artists

Artworks

Glossary

A

abstract A style of art that does not show a realistic subject. Abstract art usually includes geometric shapes, bold colors, and lines.

actual lines Lines that are real, not imaginary.

additive method A technique for creating a three-dimensional artwork in which materials, such as clay or found objects, are added or assembled.

aerial perspective A technique used to create the illusion of air and space in an artwork. Close-up objects are bright and consist of darker colors; faraway objects and air consist of muted colors and large portions of white. Also known as *atmospheric perspective.*

altered proportion A technique used by an artist to change the size relationship of shapes in an artwork. See *monumental* and *miniature.*

alternating rhythm Rhythm created in an artwork by repeating two or more elements on a regular, interchanging basis.

analogous [ə na′ lə gəs] Colors that appear next to each other on the color wheel. Analogous colors have one hue in common. For example, blue, blue-green, and blue-violet all contain blue. Also known as *related colors.*

applied art Artworks that are functional. Also known as *utilitarian art.*

appliqué [a plə kā′] A design created by sewing pieces of cloth onto a larger cloth background.

aqueduct A channel or conduit built for transporting water from a distant source.

archaeologist A person who studies past human life and culture by the recovery and examination of remaining material evidence, such as graves, buildings, tools, and pottery.

architect An artist who plans and designs buildings and other structures.

architectural plans Plans developed by an architect in order to guide the construction of a building or structure.

architecture The art and science of designing buildings and other structures.

armature [är′ mə chùr] A skeletal framework or support for a sculpture.

art media The materials used by artists to create artworks.

art teacher A specialist in the field of visual art who teaches and helps students and others understand and participate in the world of visual arts and ideas.

artwork A term that refers to any artistic object or production.

assemblage [ə sem′ blij] An additive sculpture often made of recycled objects that assume new meaning within the artwork.

asymmetrical balance [ā sə me′ tri kal] A type of balance in which the two sides of an artwork look equally important even though they are not alike. Also known as *informal balance.*

asymmetrical composition The uneven arrangement of elements of art in a unified artwork, such as a landscape.

atmospheric perspective A technique used to create the illusion of air and space in an artwork. Close-up objects are bright and consist of darker colors; faraway objects and air consist of muted colors and large portions of white. Also known as *aerial perspective.*

B

background The part of an artwork that appears the farthest away.

balance The arrangement of the parts of an artwork to give a sense of overall equality in visual weight. Balance can be symmetrical, asymmetrical, or radial. Balance is a principle of design.

bas-relief A type of relief sculpture in which objects or forms project only slightly from a background. Also known as *low-relief.*

batik [bə tēk′] An art form in which dye and wax are used to make pictures or patterns on cloth.

binder A material, such as wax, egg, glue, resin, or oil, that binds together the coloring grains and powder in a pigment.

bird's-eye view A view shown from above. For example, a photograph of a town taken from an airplane provides a bird's-eye view.

blending A shading technique that changes the value of a color little by little.

block In printmaking, a piece of flat material, such as wood or metal, with a design on the surface, which is a mirror image of the composition that will appear as a print. The block is used to print the design. (See also *plate.*) In sculpture, a solid material, such as wood or stone, used for carving.

blueprint A photographic print used to copy the final drawing of a plan for building something.

brayer [brā′ ər] In printmaking, a rubber roller used to evenly spread ink over a surface, such as a printing block or plate.

bust A sculpted portrait or representation consisting of the head and part of the shoulders of a person.

C

canon A set of principles, rules, standards, or norms.

caricature [kar′ i kə chür] An artwork that exaggerates the features or aspects of a person or object, usually in a humorous way.

cartoonist An artist who draws cartoons for newspapers, magazines, and other print media.

carving A subtractive method of sculpting requiring the sculptor to cut or chip away pieces from a block of material, such as wood, stone, or other hard material.

casting A sculpting process in which a liquid, such as molten bronze or liquid plaster, is poured into a heat-proof mold to create a three-dimensional form or an impression.

ceramics The art of making objects from clay and hardening them with fire. Also, artworks made by this process.

cityscape Artwork that gives a view of a city.

Classic A style whose focus is on perfection of form, with an emphasis on harmony and unity, in useful and attractive designs.

coiling In basket making, to wind the material in concentric rings and spirals.

collage [kə läzh′] An artwork in which the artist glues bits of cut or torn paper, photographs, fabric, or other materials to a flat surface.

color The visual quality of objects caused by the amount of light reflected by them. Color is an element of art. See *hue*.

color scheme A plan for combining colors in a work of art.

complementary Colors that contrast with one another. Complementary colors are opposite one another on the color wheel.

composition The plan, placement, or arrangement of the elements of art in an artwork. Composition may also refer to any work of art.

computer animation The art and process of using a computer to create moving images and characters.

computer arts Artworks created through the use of computer technology as a medium.

conservator [kən sər′ va tər] A person who works to protect artworks from damage and decay.

contrast The difference between two unlike things, such as a light color and a dark color.

converging lines Actual or implied lines that move toward an intersecting point in space.

cool colors The family of colors that includes greens, blues, and violets. Cool colors bring to mind cool things, places, and feelings.

crafts Useful or decorative artworks created by hand, such as quilts, baskets, ceramics, jewelry, and furniture.

creative process The process of inventive and imaginative expression through the use of art materials and tools.

cropping To trim a photograph or image to reduce its size or change emphasis.

cross-hatching A shading technique using lines that cross each other.

Cubism An abstract art style developed by Pablo Picasso and Georges Braque in the twentieth century in which the subject is divided into shapes and forms which are then recombined so that each part of the subject is shown from a different point of view.

cuneiform [kyù nē′ a fòrm] A system of writing used in ancient Mesopotamia, in which the characters are wedge-shaped.

curator A person who does research for a museum. Curators recommend artworks for the museum to consider purchasing. They also select artworks for display from the museum's permanent collection.

curriculum A course of study offered by a school.

D

decorative art Handicrafts that result in beautiful, useful objects. Rug and fabric design, furniture-making, and glassblowing are all decorative arts.

depth The use of the techniques of perspective and overlapping to show deep space on a two-dimensional plane.

design The creative and organized arrangement of lines, shapes, spaces, colors, forms, textures, and other elements in an artwork. Also, the act of planning and arranging the parts of an artwork.

detail A small part of a larger artwork enlarged for closer viewing. Also, a minute or particularly interesting part of an artwork.

developing techniques Techniques applied during the chemical process of rendering a photographic image from film into print, often used to create certain effects.

diagonal A slanted edge or line.

diagram A plan, sketch, drawing or outline designed to demonstrate or explain how something works or to clarify the relationship between the parts of a whole.

digital technology Technology which converts visual images into binary code through the use of items such as digital cameras, video and audio recorders, scanners, or computers.

docent [dō′ sənt] A person who gives information and conducts tours in a museum. Many docents are trained volunteers.

dominance A way to show emphasis in an artwork in which one element or object in the composition is visually the strongest or most important part of the work.

E

elements of art The basic parts and symbols of an artwork. The elements of art are line, color, value, shape, texture, form, and space.

elevation A scale drawing that shows one side of a structure.

emphasis [em(p)′fə səs] Importance given to certain objects or areas in an artwork. Color, texture, shape, space, placement, and size can be used to create dominance, contrast, or a focal point. Emphasis is a principle of design.

etching A printing process in which a design is drawn into wax-covered metal plate. The plate is then bathed in acid, which eats the metal on the areas unprotected by the wax. The wax is removed and ink is applied to the etched surface. The plate is then pressed onto a surface to reveal the print. Also, a print made by this process. See *intaglio print*.

Expressionism A style of artwork developed in the twentieth century that expresses a definite or strong mood or feeling through simple designs and brilliant colors.

F

facade [fə säd′] The front, or main face, of a building.

fine art Artworks that are created for the sole purpose of being viewed.

floor plan The arrangement of rooms inside a building.

focal point A way to show emphasis in an artwork in which the artist sets an element apart from the others to create a visual center of interest.

foreground The part of an artwork that seems nearest.

form A three-dimensional object, such as a cube or ball, or the representation of a three-dimensional object, defined by contour, height, depth, and width. Form is an element of art.

G

geometric forms Forms such as the sphere, cube, and pyramid, whose contours represent a circle, square, and triangle, respectively.

geometric shapes Precise, mathematical shapes, such as the circle, square, triangle, oval, and rectangle.

gesture A motion of the limbs or body made to express or help express a thought or to emphasize speech.

graphic design The art of communicating through images and lettering, mostly for commercial purposes, such as logos, letterheads, packages, advertisements, posters, signs, books, Web pages, and other publications.

graphic designer An artist who creates visual communications and messages through images and letters.

graphic style The individual way a graphic artist expresses himself or herself.

H

hatching A shading technique using thin parallel lines.

home fashions Furniture, fabrics, decorations, and wall art used by interior designers to decorate a home.

horizon line The line created in an artwork by the meeting of sky and ground, usually at the viewer's eye level.

horizontal line In an artwork, a line that runs side-to-side, parallel to the horizon. Horizontal lines can appear peaceful and calm.

hue [hyü] Another word for color.

human-made environment A person's or organism's circumstances or surroundings made by humans rather than occurring in nature.

I

illustration A design or picture in a book, magazine, or other print or electronic medium that visually explains the text or shows what happens in a story.

illustrator An artist who creates designs and pictures for books, magazines, or other print or electronic media.

implied lines Lines that are not real, but suggested by the placement of other lines, shapes, and colors.

Impressionism An art movement and style developed in the last 1800s by a group of French artists. Artists of the Impressionist style drew and painted their impressions of visual reality by showing the effects of light and color on everyday objects.

Impressionist Of, relating to, or practicing Impressionism.

industrial design The design of objects created and sold by industry, such as automobiles, appliances, and telephones.

industrial designer An artist who plans and designs functional objects that are most often mass produced, such as appliances, toys, and automobiles.

Industrial Revolution A period of technological, socioeconomic, and cultural changes that began in England in the eighteenth century, and which spread to other parts of the world. The changes brought about the use of new building materials, energy sources, new machinery, factories, transportation and communication, and the further development of science and industry.

installation An artwork that is assembled for a specific space for public viewing. Some installations are permanent, while others are temporary.

intaglio print [in tal′ yō] A print that results from a technique in which the image to be printed is cut or scratched into a surface or plate.

intensity The brightness or dullness of a hue. A hue mixed with its complement is less intense than the pure color.

interior designer An artist who plans the layout and design of interior rooms and spaces.

intermediate color A color that is a mixture of a primary and a secondary color that are next to each other on the color wheel. Blue-green, red-orange, and red-violet are examples of intermediate colors.

International Style A modernist style of architecture that appeared in Europe between 1920 and 1930 characterized by regular, unadorned geometric forms, open interiors, and the use of glass, steel, and reinforced concrete.

K

keep The strongest, most important tower in a castle.

kylix [kî⁄ liks] An ancient Greek drinking cup with a wide shallow bowl, a pair of horizontal handles, a slender stem, and a small base.

L

landscape A drawing or painting that shows an outdoor scene or scenery, such as trees, lakes, mountains, and fields.

landscape designer An artist who uses plants, rocks, trees, and other materials to design and create pleasing and functional outdoor spaces. Also known as a *landscape architect.*

layout The arrangement of letters and images on a page.

line A mark on a surface usually created by a pen, pencil, or brush. Lines vary in width, length, direction, color, and degree of curve, and can be actual or implied. Line is an element of art.

linear perspective A technique that makes use of actual and implied lines to create the illusion of depth on a two-dimensional surface. If the lines in an artwork created with this technique are extended, they converge at a point that represents the eye level of the viewer. This point is called the vanishing point.

line quality The special character of any line, such as thick or thin, smooth or rough, continuous or broken.

lithograph A type of print made by drawing a design on a metal or stone plate using a greasy substance. The plate is washed with water, and then covered with greasy ink that adheres only to the design and not the wet surface of the plate. The plate is then pressed onto paper.

logo A design created by a graphic artist as a symbol to visually represent a business, club, city, or other group.

loom A frame or machine used to hold yarn, or other fibers, for weaving.

M

media Materials used to create artworks, such as clay or paint. The singular of media is *medium*.

Medieval period The period of European history that followed the fall of the Western Roman Empire. Also known as the *Middle Ages* or *Dark Ages*.

medium A material used to create artworks, such as clay or paint. The plural of medium is *media*.

Mesolithic [me zə li⁄ thik] The period between ca. 10,000–8000 B.C., and which followed the Paleolithic period. During the Mesolithic period humans began to wander less and establish villages. The artworks of this period often include human figures as well as animals. Also known as the *Middle Stone Age*.

Middle Ages The period in European history between the fall of Rome in A.D. 410 to about 1450. Also known as the *Medieval period* and the *Dark Ages*.

middle ground In an artwork, the part between the foreground and the background.

miniature Artworks that are of smaller-than-life proportions.

mixed media Artworks that are created from more than one medium.

module Term that denotes a standardized unit of measurement, usually four inches or ten centimeters, from which all other measurements in a building, drawing, or sculpture are derived.

monochromatic [mä nə krō ma⁄ tik] A color scheme that uses different values of a single hue by showing tints and shades of the same hue.

monumental Artworks that are of larger-than-life proportions.

mood The feeling or emotion created in an artwork through the artist's use of the elements of art and principles of design. For example, warm colors may suggest a lively, sunny mood. Cool colors may suggest a peaceful, lonely, or fearful mood.

motivator One who provides incentive to or who encourages others to act or move to action or who encourages others.

mural A large artwork, usually a painting, that is applied directly onto or placed on a wall or ceiling, often in public places.

N

narrative art An artwork that tells a visual story, often about everyday life or historical events. This style was especially popular in Victorian England.

natural environment A natural setting that has not been changed by humans.

negative space The empty space around and between forms or shapes in an artwork.

Neolithic [nē ə li⁄ thik] Of or relating to the cultural period of the Stone Age ca. 8000–3000 B.C., characterized by the development of agriculture and the making of polished stone implements. Also called the *New Stone Age* .

neutral A word used for black, white, and tints and shades of gray. Some artists use tints and shades of brown as neutrals.

Non-western Art The art of parts of the world other than those included in the Western tradition that include functional art, such as ceremonial masks and costumes, cooking utensils, and tools.

O

oil-based paints Paints made from a mixture of colored pigment and linseed oil.

one-point perspective A form of linear perspective in which all lines appear to meet at a single vanishing point on the horizon.

opaque [ō pāk⁄] The quality of not letting light through; the opposite of transparent.

organic form A "free-form" which has irregular and uneven edges and is often found in nature, such as an apple, a tree, or an animal.

organic shape A "free-form" shape that is irregular and uneven, such as the shape of a leaf, a flower, or a cloud.

overlapping Partly or completely covering one shape or form with another to show space and distance in an artwork.

P

Paleolithic [pā lē ə li⁄ thik] Of or relating to the cultural period of the Stone Age beginning from about 750,000 years ago until the Mesolithic Age, about 15,000 years ago. Also called the *Old Stone Age.*

palette [pa⁄ lət] A flat board on which a painter holds and mixes color.

panorama An unbroken view of an entire surrounding area.

papier mâché [pā⁄ pər mə shā⁄] A medium used in creating forms by covering an armature or other base with strips of paper that have been soaked in watery paste, and then molding the strips. The papier mâché hardens as it dries.

parallel lines Two or more straight lines or edges on the same plane that do not intersect. Parallel lines have the same direction.

pastel [pas tel⁄] A drawing and painting medium in which pigments are mixed with gum and water, and pressed into a dried stick form for use as crayons. Works of art created with this medium are also called pastels.

pattern Repeated colors, lines, shapes, forms, or textures in an artwork. Pattern is a principle of design. Also, a plan or model to be followed when making something.

pediment In classical architecture, a triangular space at the end of a building, formed by the ends of the sloping roof and the cornice. Also, an ornamental feature having this shape.

pharaoh A ruler of ancient Egypt.

photographer An artist who uses a camera as his or her medium.

photojournalist A person who tells a news story primarily with photographs.

photomontage [fō tə män täzh′] An artwork made by combining all or parts of different photographs, often in combination with other types of graphic material.

pictographs Ancient drawings, often found on cave walls, that tell stories or record a culture's beliefs and practices.

picture plane The two-dimensional surface of a picture or drawing on which three-dimensional images are represented.

pigment A coloring material made from crushed minerals, plants, or chemicals, usually held together with a binder.

placement The act of placing or arranging elements and objects in an artwork.

plaiting [plā′ ting] In basket making, to make by braiding.

plate In printmaking, a piece of flat material, such as wood or metal, with a design on the surface. The plate is used to print the design, which is a mirror image of the composition. See also *block.*

pointillism A painting and drawing technique developed by Georges Seurat in the nineteenth century, in which tiny dots of color are applied to the canvas or drawing surface.

point of view Angle from which the viewer sees an object or a scene. The three points of view are the straight-on view, bird's-eye view, and ground-level or worm's-eye view.

political cartoon A cartoon that relates to, and usually satirizes, the structure and affairs of government, politics, or the state.

Pop Art An art style that developed in England in the 1950s and spread to the United States in the 1960s. The subjects of Pop Art include everyday, popular objects, such as product packages, comic strips, and advertisements.

positive space The space that a form or shape occupies in an artwork.

Postmodern Term used to describe the attempt to modify and extend the tradition of modernism with borrowings from the Classical style.

Prehistoric Of, relating to, or belonging to the era before recorded history.

primary color A color that cannot be mixed from other colors, but from which other colors are made. The primary colors are red, yellow, and blue.

principles of design Guidelines that artists use to organize the elements of art in a composition. Unity, variety, emphasis, balance, proportion, pattern, and rhythm are the principles of design.

printing ink A type of ink that is thicker and stickier than the ink for fountain pens and that is used in the printmaking process.

printmaking The process of transferring an image from an inked surface to another surface to create an artwork.

profile The side view of a subject.

progressive rhythm Rhythm created in an artwork by showing regular changes in a repeated element, such as a series of circles that progressively increase in size from small to large. The changes may also progress from light to dark, or from bottom to top.

proportion The relation of the parts of an artwork to each other and to the whole. Proportion is a principle of design.

R

radial balance A type of balance in which lines or shapes spread out from a center point.

red-figured style A technique used in ancient Greek pottery in which figures were left unpainted against a black background, exposing the red terra-cotta clay.

regular rhythm Rhythm in an artwork created by repeating the same element, such as a shape, without variation.

relief print The technique of printing in which an image raised from a background is inked and printed.

relief sculpture A type of sculpture in which forms project from a background and are meant to be seen from one side.

Renaissance [re nə sän(t)s⁄] The period between the 1300s and 1600s, during which new ideas and technological advances, as well as renewed interest in the classical styles of the Romans and Greeks, laid the foundation for modern art and society.

resist A process by which a material, such as wax, is used to protect parts of a surface from paint or dye.

rhythm The repetition of elements, such as lines, shapes, or colors, that creates a feeling of visual motion in an artwork. Rhythm is a principle of design. In music, rhythm refers to the pattern of a melody.

S

satire Irony, sarcasm, or caustic wit used to attack or expose folly, vice, or stupidity.

scale The size of an object in relation to an ideal or standard size.

sculpture An artwork made by modeling, carving, casting, or joining materials into a three-dimensional form. Clay, wood, stone, and metal are often used to make sculptures.

sculpture in the round A sculpture that is fashioned to be viewed from all sides. Also known as *full round*.

seascape An artwork that represents the sea, ocean, or shore.

secondary color A color made by mixing two primary colors. The secondary colors are orange, violet, and green.

self-portrait An artwork that shows the likeness of the artist who created it.

shade A color made by adding black to a hue. For example, adding black to green results in dark green. Also, the darkness of a color value. See *value*.

shading A way of showing gradual changes in lightness or darkness in a drawing or painting. Shading helps make a picture look more three-dimensional.

shape A two-dimensional area created by connecting actual or implied lines. A shape can be geometric, such as a circle or square, or organic, having an irregular outline. Shape is an element of art.

simulated Made in resemblance of or as a substitute for another.

size relationships A technique that alters the proportions of compositions. The three categories are monumental, miniature, and exaggerated.

sketchbook A book or pad of blank paper used for drawing and keeping sketches.

slip A soupy mixture of clay and water that acts as glue to join scored pieces of clay.

software Computer applications used for various functions, such as drawing, Web design, editing text, creating graphics, or altering images.

solvent A liquid, such as turpentine or water, used to control the thickness or thinness of paint.

space The area around, above, between, inside, or below objects. Positive space is the area occupied by an object. Negative space is the empty area surrounding an object. Space is an element of art.

standard proportion That which appears appropriate in height, width, and depth compared to its surroundings. The human body is considered to be the standard by which the size or proportion of other objects is measured.

still life An artwork showing an arrangement of objects that cannot move on their own, such as fruit, foods, bottles, books, or cut flowers.

still photography The art and science of making a picture with a camera and film other than a motion picture or video camera.

stippling A shading technique creating dark values by applying a dot pattern.

stitchery A term for artwork created with a needle, thread or yarn, and cloth, such as a quilt.

straight-on view Point of view, usually at eye level, that encourages a viewer to focus on other aspects of a composition.

study A preparatory drawing, often in preparation for a larger artwork.

subject A person, animal, object, or scene represented in an artwork; the topic of an artwork.

subtractive method A technique used in creating three-dimensional artworks in which materials, such as clay, stone, or plaster, are removed or carved away.

symbol A letter, color, sign, or picture that represents words, messages, or ideas, such as thoughts and feelings. For example, a red heart is often used as a symbol for love.

symmetrical balance [sə me′ tri kəl] A type of balance in which both sides of an artwork look the same or almost the same. Also known as *formal balance.*

symmetrical composition The even, balanced arrangement of elements of art in a unified artwork, such as a landscape or still life.

T

tactile texture A texture you can feel with your hands, such as rough or smooth. Also known as *actual texture.*

teaching strategies Plans of action used to teach a particular subject.

technique The way an artist uses and applies art media and tools to create a certain type of artwork.

tempera paint A chalky, water-based paint that is thick and opaque. Also known as *poster paint.*

textile An artwork made from cloth or fibers, such as yarn.

texture The way something feels to the touch (actual texture) or how it may look (visual texture). Texture is an element of art.

tint A light value of a color, such as pink, that is created by mixing a hue with white. Also, the lightness of a color value. See *value.*

topographic landscape A landscape in which the surface features are manipulated to create a design.

transparent The quality of letting light pass through; the opposite of opaque.

triptych [trip′ tik] A picture or carving in three panels.

twining In basket making, the technique of twisting, intertwining, or interlacing fibers.

two-point perspective A form of linear perspective in which all lines appear to meet at either of two vanishing points on the horizon.

U

unity The quality of seeming whole and complete, when all the parts of an artwork look right together. Unity is a principle of design.

urban designer An architect who specializes in the planning of a city.

utilitarian Designed for a specific, functional purpose. Also known as *applied art*.

V

value The lightness or darkness of a color. Tints have a light value. Shades have a dark value. Value is an element of art.

vanishing point In linear perspective, the place on the horizon where parallel lines seem to meet or converge.

variety The use or combination of elements of art, such as line, shape, or color, to provide interest in an artwork. Variety is a principle of design.

vertical line In an artwork, a line that runs up and down, such as a flagpole or a giant redwood tree. Vertical lines appear strong and powerful.

videography [vi dē ä′ grə fē] The art or practice of using a video camera.

visual composition The arrangement of elements in a photograph or landscape.

visual narrative A series of pictures that tell a story, often in video or film.

visual texture The way a surface appears through the sense of vision. For example, the surface of a sculpture may appear shiny or dull. Also known as *simulated texture*.

W

warm colors The family of colors that includes reds, yellows, and oranges. Warm colors bring to mind warm things, places, and feelings.

warp In weaving, the vertical threads attached to the top and bottom of a loom.

water-based paints Water-soluble paints, such as tempera, watercolor, or acrylic, that use different binders and have different qualities.

weaving A process of interlocking thread, yarn, or other fibers to create a fabric, usually on a loom.

Web design Design specializing in the development of a home page on the World Wide Web for a person, group, or organization.

weft The threads that cross over and under the warp fibers on a loom.

Index

Acknowledgments

Illustrations

19, 23, 27, 31, 35, 43, 47, 51, 55, 57, 107, 111, 115, 119, 127, 131, 135, 139, 143, 147, 149, 151, 159, 163, 167, 171, 179, 183, 187, 191, 193 Chris Notarile

67, 71, 75, 79, 83, 91, 95, 97, 203, 207, 211, 215, 219, 226, 227, 231, 235, 239, 243, 245, 255, 259, 263, 275, 279, 283, 287, 289, 012, 013 SuLing Wang

Photographs

Every effort has been made to secure permission and provide appropriate credit for photographic material. The publisher deeply regrets any omission and pledges to correct errors called to its attention in subsequent editions.

Unless otherwise acknowledged, all photographs are the property of Scott Foresman, a division of Pearson Education.

Photo locators denoted as follows: Top (t), Center (c), Bottom (b), Left (l), Right (r), Background (Bkgd)

Front Matter
Page iv, © Rudi Von Briel/PhotoEdit; 1(tr), © Gemaldegalerie, Munich/SuperStock; 2, M.C. Escher's "Rippled Surface" © 2003/Cordon Art B.V—Baarn—Holland. All rights reserved; 2(t), © Explorer, Paris/SuperStock; 2(b), © Gilbert Mayers/ SuperStock; 3, © Steve Vidler/SuperStock; 4(bl), Bequest of Marion Koogler McNay/Collection of the McNay Art Museum. © Fiduciario en el Fideicomiso relativo a los Museos Diego Rivera y Frida Kahlo. Reproduction authorized by the Bank of Mexico, Mexico City; 5(tr), Ashmolean Museum, Oxford; 5(br), Photo by Paul Macapia/Gift of Virginia and Bagley Wright/Seattle Art Museum; 6(t), © Ansel Adams Publishing Rights Trust/Corbis; 7, Mary Ann Sullivan; 7(tr), Commisioned by Su Stanton/ Photoreaserch Inc./Michael Bartalos; 8(b), © Richard Cummins/Corbis; 8(t), The Georgia O'Keeffe Museum, Santa Fe/Art Resource, NY. © 2004 The Georgia O'Keeffe Foundation/Artists Rights Society (ARS), New York; 9, © Smithsonian American Art Museum, Washington, D.C./Art Resource, NY; 10(t), Courtesy of Nedra Matteucci Galleries; 10(c), © Roger Wood/Corbis; 10(b), © David Butow/Corbis; 11(br), © Getty Images.

Units 1–6
Page 14, © Gianni Dagli Orti/Corbis; 15, © Scala/ Art Resource, NY; 16, © Getty Images; 16, © Javier Pierini/Getty Images; 17, The National Gallery, Olso/Corbis; 7, © Burnstein Collection/Corbis; 18, © Christie's Images/Corbis; 20, © Getty Images; 20, © Edmond von Hoorick/Getty Images; 21, © The Art Institute of Chicago. Alfred Stieglitz Collection, gift of Georgie O'Keeffe, 1969.835. Reproduction © The Art Institute of Chicago. © 2004 The Georgia O'Keeffe Foundation/Artists Rights Society (ARS), New York; 22, Gift of Bruce Allyn Eissner, Class of 1965, and Judith Pick Eissner. 80.63.5. Courtesy of The Herbert F. Johnson Museum of Art, Cornell University. © 2004 Succession H. Matisse, Paris/Artists Rights Society (ARS), New York; 24, © P.J. Wagner/Photo Access/Getty Images; 24, © Corbis; 25(b), Hirshhorn Museum and Sculpture Garden, Smithsonian Institution, Gift of Joseph H. Hirshhorn, 1974 (74.1). © Henry Moore Foundation; 26, Photograph by David Wharton, courtesy of the Modern Art Museum of Fort Worth; 28, © Christie's Images/Corbis; 28, © Getty Images; 28(r), © Christie's Images/Corbis 29, © Pennsylvania Academy of Fine Art/Corbis; © Anna Belle Lee Washington/SuperStock; 32(b), © SuperStock; 33, © Worcester Art Museum, Massachusetts/Bridgeman Art Library; 34, © The Newark Museum/Art Resource, NY; 36, © Scala/Art Resource, NY; 37(t), © Mary Evans Picture Library; 37(ct), © Bettmann/ Corbis; 37(cb), © AFP/Corbis; 37(b), © Gianni Dagli Orti/Corbis; 38, © Bettmann/ Corbis; 39(b), © National Gallery, Parma, Italy/ Giraudon, Paris/SuperStock; 39(t), © Erich Lessing/ Art Resource, NY; 40(b), The Museum of Fine Arts,

Back Matter